FRANCIS LEE JAQUES
ARTIST-NATURALIST

PUBLISHED BY THE
UNIVERSITY OF MINNESOTA PRESS, MINNEAPOLIS
FOR THE
JAMES FORD BELL MUSEUM OF NATURAL HISTORY

FRANCIS LEE JAQUES
ARTIST-NATURALIST

DONALD T. LUCE & LAURA M. ANDREWS

with excerpts from F. L. Jaques's manuscript autobiography

To the late Junius Bird, Curator Emeritus of South American Archaeology at the American Museum of Natural History.

Copyright © 1982 by the University of Minnesota
All rights reserved.
Published by the University of Minnesota Press,
2037 University Avenue Southeast, Minneapolis MN 55414
Printed in the United States of America

ISBN: 0-8166-1145-9 hc
        0-8166-1146-7 pbk

The University of Minnesota
is an equal-opportunity
educator and employer.

Foreword

Francis Lee Jaques was the first bird artist I ever knew. Indeed, I had never met an ornithologist of any sort when I boarded the train for New York City to attend my first convention of the American Ornithologists' Union in 1925.

Arriving a day early, I found my way to the American Museum of Natural History, the fine old institution on 79th Street and Central Park West, which pioneered the art of the diorama or habitat display. Outstanding at that time was a great oval dome from which a wedge of geese and an assortment of other flying birds were suspended by invisible wires. Above them flew other flocks, painted with deceptive realism against a painted sky. I was enthralled by this "sky-o-rama" overhead.

Wandering into an adjacent hall, I found a youngish man in shirtsleeves hanging bird paintings for the A.O.U. exhibit. To make conversation, I asked: "Did Bruce Horsfall paint that ceiling in the other room?"

"Oh, I did that," was his offhand, self-effacing reply.

The artist-preparator with the hammer and picture wire was "Lee" Jaques. He had been hired only the year before by Dr. Frank M. Chapman, the museum's Curator of Birds, who at that time was the father figure of American ornithology.

Chapman, who conceived the diorama idea, a new concept in museum exhibits, had discovered that most bird artists, no matter how skilled, tended to paint their birds *against* the landscape rather than *into* it, surrounded by light and air. Even Fuertes, the most celebrated of all bird portraitists, failed to achieve the third-dimensional feeling, the movement in space, required by the habitat groups. When Chapman heard of Jaques, who was making a name for himself in Minnesota, he quickly hired him after seeing several of his canvases of waterfowl.

His first assignment was the dome of the bird hall which he painted from a high scaffold—rather like Michaelangelo in the Sistine Chapel. During his years in New York, Jaques was to paint more than half of the dioramas in the American Museum, leaving a greater visual stamp on that institution than any other person, before or since. Other habitat groups, some of his finest, grace the halls of the Bell Museum in Minneapolis, the Peabody Museum in New Haven, and the Museum of Science in Boston.

Jaques brought the diorama to its highest degree of development. He approached each habitat group as a problem in engineering disguised by artistry. He was skilled at handling perspective on a curved surface. Although he would sometimes study photographs, he preferred to make preliminary sketches in the field, commenting that he did not intend to produce "large Kodachromes." He worked out his own system of landscape notation. Sketching quickly in pencil, he then used numbers coded to a color chart to indicate color values.

Whereas the dioramas by their very nature were intended to "fool the eye," his canvases were freed from this restraint; they were more decorative. The innovative branchwork of the trees, the reflections in the water, the sweep of the clouds and the sky always bore the unmistakable Jaques imprint.

Whereas the color values in his canvases often tended toward pastel shades, his black-and-white scratchboard drawings had a bolder, almost stark look. Several books written by his wife and inseparable companion, Florence Page Jaques, were illustrated by Lee. Other artists, enamored of his fine sense of abstraction and his inventiveness, have tried to imitate his scratchboard style with varying degrees of success. But they have seldom achieved the dynamic balance between white spaces, mass, and line that Jaques had mastered. His bold knife work in his shading may have been dictated by the tendency of inks to fill in the more delicate white lines when a drawing was reproduced by zinc line cut.

Although Francis Lee Jaques lived in New York City for many years and traveled a great deal, he felt most at home in Minnesota, where the duck prairies meet the North Woods. His dioramas and canvases are a sensitive and joyous celebration of the wild world—a record of the way it was in his time.

Roger Tory Peterson

Preface

In the mid 1960s Francis Lee Jaques (pronounced "Jay-quees"), having decided to leave some record of his life, began to write an autobiography. For years his wife Florence had written about their travels and adventures as they explored together the natural areas across North America. Lee had illustrated these books and articles with his famous scratchboard drawings, and a productive and successful partnership had developed. Their friends were thus somewhat surprised that he now wanted to write. He felt strongly, however, that there were aspects of his life that he needed to write about, and he was determined to document them.

Once a week, Lee and Florence met with Pat and Thomas Young, their friends and neighbors, and read the chapter or so that Lee had written during the previous week. Criticisms and suggestions were made but very rarely did he change anything. Although the manuscript grew week by week, when Lee died in 1969 the autobiography was still in a rough hand-written form.

Florence considered it her responsibility to finish the project. She first attempted to prepare Lee's manuscript for publication, but had to give up: their writing styles were simply incompatible. Instead, she wrote a biography in her own words, based on information from Lee's manuscript as well as her own experience from their years together. Florence had great skill with words; it was her craft as Lee's craft was painting and drawing. Her book, *Francis Lee Jaques, Artist of the Wilderness World*, is a tribute to her dedication, and will doubtless remain the best account of the life of this remarkable man.

Our intention here is to present a biographical view of Francis Lee Jaques through his own words and pictures. We have taken sections of his autobiography and combined them with his pictures, both sketches and finished works, which complement the text. In his autobiography, Lee stresses parts of his life that are not emphasized elsewhere. He discusses his life as a museum artist and his experiences on many far-flung scientific expeditions. Included are many of his personal observations of natural history and views on conservation that are important in understanding him as an artist-naturalist, as well as a unique individual.

We have endeavored to place Lee's works in the perspective not only of developments in wildlife painting, but also in relation to the times in which he lived. His life from 1887 to 1969 spans several great transitions in American culture. In his youth, he experienced the last of the pioneer era on farms in Kansas and Minnesota. As a railroad fireman and electrician in northern Minnesota, he traded the isolation and deprivations of a wilderness farmstead for the grueling and dangerous life of an early industrial worker. Eventually, his drive to express the poignant beauty he saw in the wilderness around him led to a serious artistic career. With his move in 1924 to the American Museum of Natural History in New York, he was swept into the center of modern urban culture. Here, he saw the evolution of the conservation movement, from its first campaigns against market hunting in the early twentieth century, to the emergence of popular ecological activism in the 1960s.

These events were part of him, deeply affecting his work, and he reflects upon them in his autobiography. His words are plain and unpolished. They were those of a man in his late seventies, reminiscing about his life, occasionally rambling on in a stream-of-consciousness manner. But just as a sketch often reveals things about the artist not seen in a finished work, these excerpts from his autobiography contain some of the flavor of Lee's character not otherwise found. They are often rough as hand-hewn timbers, but this seems wholly appropriate for a man whose character was cut on the American frontier.

This book is published in conjunction with an exhibition that has the same title. Organized by the James Ford Bell Museum of Natural History, the exhibition will travel to museums across North America. The artwork reproduced here and in the exhibition is drawn largely from the collection bequeathed to the Bell Museum by Florence and substantially enlarged by donations from their many friends. Lee's artistry and Florence's writing made a significant contribution to the public understanding and appreciation of our natural heritage. We hope that the publication of this book and the wider exposure of his work through the exhibition will help further this cause.

Acknowledgments

This book and the accompanying exhibition would not have been possible without the cooperation and assistance of many individuals and museums throughout the country. We would like to express our gratitude to the staff members of the James Ford Bell Museum of Natural History who have helped in this endeavor in countless ways, particularly Robert C. Bright and Harrison B. Tordoff who directed our efforts. We are also grateful for the valuable assistance received from the staff of the University of Minnesota Gallery.

We are grateful for the numerous suggestions on the manuscript we received from Robert Larson, the late Junius Bird, Rusk and Lucinda Anderson, Robert Askins, Donald Eckelberry, Roger Tory Peterson, and John Fitzpatrick, among others. Cecil Reichert of the California Academy of Sciences provided invaluable assistance in locating photographs of Jaques taken on the *Zaca* expedition of 1934-35. Stephen Quinn, Mary Le Croy and Landis Smith of the American Museum of Natural History, and Eleanor Stickney and Copeland McClintock of the Peabody Museum at Yale were kind enough to make the Jaques materials in their collections available for our use. Both institutions undertook restoration work of Jaques paintings in order that they could be used in the exhibition. Alexander Hoffman of Doubleday has given us his willing assistance and supportive enthusiasm, a most necessary constant throughout this project.

We are, of course, indebted to all the individuals and institutions that have generously lent Jaques artwork for the exhibition and allowed their reproduction here. We would like to recognize the generosity of Kent Day Coes, Clarence Cottom, Mrs. Franz Feger, Mr. and Mrs. Malvin Herz, Louis W. Hill, Jr., the late Florence Page Jaques, Charlotte Johnson, Mrs. Leta F. Monninger, Mrs. William Morden, Colleen and Carl Nelson, and the late Sigurd F. Olson, who have donated Jaques artwork to the Bell Museum Collection. Our special thanks to Patricia and Thomas Young, Arnold Bolz, Walter Breckenridge, Peggy Azad, Clayton Rudd, and the many other friends of the Jaques who shared their time and memories and gave us encouragement along the way.

Illustrations

FRANCIS LEE JAQUES
ARTIST-NATURALIST

2

The Travels of Lee and Florence Jaques
Lee probably painted this map in the late 1940s, and, as he and Florence continued their travels, added more lines. Painted in the bottom corners are the schooners *Morrissey* and *Zaca*, the covered wagon in which Lee came to Minnesota, and a selection of his cars, canoes, trains, and other means of transport.

EVERYONE HAS TO BE born sometime, I suppose. Anyway I was—on September 28, 1887, in a house owned by my grandfather. The house was a small two-story affair on a large lot bordered on the back by the Rock Island Railway—double track—which had been completed only about 25 years before. A very busy railroad.

With these words, Francis Lee Jaques began his autobiography, mentioning a railroad in practically the same breath as his birth. The place was Geneseo, Illinois, a small midwestern town where Lee lived with his father, Ephraim Parker Jaques, and his mother, Emma Jane (Monninger) Jaques. Next door was his grandfather's cooper shop where white-ash butter tubs were made. Lee's father was an avid hunter and a good shot, and when he wasn't out "hunting or guiding or doing something else he helped at the cooper shop."

By the time I was started in school, when I was seven, I had learned the letters of the alphabet from box cars. Maybe I could read a little, I'm not sure. It wasn't a happy time. I was the outsider, the prey of the neighborhood boys who made going to school a trial. One day I escaped and got home first, and gathered up some rocks—I was good with rocks—and hid behind one of the big maples. This boy I hated most came by and I let drive with a rock, hitting him behind the ear and inflicting an appreciable wound. It was spring and the ground was a slippery mud on the surface. During the chase that followed I saw a cap which I supposd was his, and stamped it into the mud. It was my cap.

But the war was over, and I could go to school in peace. I took drawing lessons—with crayons—in which we used 'stumps,' rolled soft gray paper somewhat sharpened at the ends, to blend the crayon. How much these lessons helped, I don't know. I don't recall that I ever had lessons in perspective. I drew Santa and his reindeer across the front blackboard in school, and political drawings on my grandfather's shop. An early drawing of the Unitarian Church in Geneseo which I still have . . . is a rather accurate perspective drawing from which the church can be easily identified. [It] has my name in grand block letters lying on the lawn. A newspaper clipping that accompanies this says I was seven [sic] years old. I *must* have been older than that. . . . But I was doing cartoons of the Spanish American War when I was eleven. I knew all the answers then.

In 1899, Ephraim Jaques moved his family to Elmo, Kansas, to try his hand at farming near the Monninger relatives. Lee was twelve and much of his education then centered on farming.

When the hay was cut and after it had dried somewhat, it was raked into windrows. The old wooden hay rake was a well-balanced machine on which one rode. Its long spring-steel tines picked up the hay and it was dumped easily by a lever. When steel began to be used in manufacture,

4

Unitarian Church
pencil sketch, 11 x 15,
c. 1894.

Done on a desk-top blotter
now badly aged, this drawing and a newspaper clip-
ping have survived from
Jaques's childhood in
Geneseo, Illinois.

pride in design was gone – the steel hayrake was dumped noisily and
awkwardly by horsepower, and something was lost. The poetry was
gone. . . .
The hay in the windrows was piled, with the pitchfork, into hay cocks,
rounded piles, which would, in part, shed water, and from these piles on
wagons, to the stack. Someone had to be on the hayrack to load it so the
hay would stay there, and someone had to pitch it up. Walking around
on soft hay – either on the rack, or the stack, and in a hay mow is no pic-
nic.
Grandfather usually put me on the hay stack. Obviously anyone's
education should consist of knowing how to make a stack, and it was an
art, of a sort.

Although farming occupied most of the daylight hours, hunting remained his father's real interest. Lee was now old enough to
accompany him, and they spent a great deal of time stalking
waterfowl that were still plentiful in the prairie marshes and
creeks.

About a mile and a half away was "Sealock's pond" and at daylight each
morning either Father or I were there to harvest what ducks we could.
Great adventure – first there was a creek which we followed. If no ducks
jumped from the creek we peeked over the dam, and if there were ducks,
got what we could. They were food, and we ate them.
Two of the first ducks I shot, a mated pair, were kept so long while I
was doing a drawing of them they spoiled. I wept, since I'd wasted them.

In Kansas, the subject of Lee's drawings changed from trains
and churches to ducks and other wildlife. The drawing of the pair
of bagged Wood Ducks is from this period. It shows how Lee ap-
plied his slight training in charcoal drawing to his newfound in-

terest in waterfowl. His early hunting experience was to affect his view of nature throughout his life.

> Duck hunting in Kansas, as we did it: I got up before daylight and was at the pond, or whatever the objective, by the time it was light enough to shoot. The excitement, the anticipation of these early mornings was greater, far greater, than any hunting ever was later. . . . From about age 11 or 12 until my early 20s guns and shooting were my primary interest. That takes care of my juvenile delinquency years. But I was not irresponsible with a gun or with what I shot. Father was very strict.
>
> In 1924 my active shooting ended, except for bits. I haven't shot anything since 1944, when we were getting material for 'Showshoe Country' at Gunflint [Lake]. . . . But my early shooting was a great assistance in painting wildlife in later years. I became familiar with the construction of wings—the feathers and the anatomy. [Later, I learned from the] dead specimens brought down from the Zoo to the Museum [in New York City] (usually on Friday afternoons, since the Zoo didn't want to entertain the dead specimen over the weekend).
>
> Game birds early taught me evolution, simply by my comparing say, the similarity between the wings of a shoveler and of a Blue-winged Teal.

As Florence writes, these experiences in Kansas are where Lee first became aware of the beauty of wildlife. "There were more

Bagged Wood Ducks
pastel, 10 x 8½,
c. 1900.

The Cloud
oil on canvas, 30 x 24,
1960s.

Late in his life, Lee Jaques
painted this portrait of
himself as a boy of twelve or
thirteen resting near his
plow on the Kansas prairie.
It expresses the wonder of
youth that led him to study
the wildlife around him, as
well as the great open skies
he would later paint so well.

varieties of birds there and great numbers of many
species. . . . Lee's greatest excitement came from the movement of single birds or flocks, and he noticed and remembered
with great accuracy the flight characteristics of each species.
(Jaques, Florence, *Francis Lee Jaques: Artist of the Wilderness
World*, p. 6).

Ephraim Jaques, besides being a great hunter and out-
doorsman, wrote articles about his experiences for *Field and
Stream*, *Sports Afield*, and other magazines. In 1902, Lee sent a
few of his drawings to *Field and Stream* with one of his father's
manuscripts. The drawings were accepted, but Lee never

thought this foretold a future career. Nevertheless, his interest in birds and nature grew and whether hunting or farming, he turned his senses to the natural world around him.

> While cultivating corn here I made my first ornithological observation. Doves nested on the ground in the absence of a better place, and I was continually plowing up the nests. If I saw the nest soon enough, and could put it back *exactly* where it was before, the doves would return to it. If I didn't get it back exactly right, they didn't return. Now this was in a large field where there was a hill of corn every three feet or so, in all directions. This area, after cultivation, looked entirely different even to the very adjacent hill of corn, since even the corn would have been tumbled askew, and there simply were no landmarks, yet the birds knew to the inch where their nest had been.

During this time Lee observed an event that would fascinate him the rest of his life and become the theme of many of his paintings: the mass migration of waterfowl.

> The hunting season must have ended, because I can't believe we would have stopped shooting while the birds were there. Nevertheless, I can remember going out along a shallow prairie stream on a Sunday afternoon, and seeing a good many ducks.

As the afternoon turned to evening, more ducks and geese passed, hundreds, then thousands in long, wavy lines flying south.

> It was my first just good, clear bird walk and I was fascinated.

After several years, it was clear that Ephraim Jaques was not going to be a success as a Kansas farmer, and he began to consider moving his family once again.

> Father had talked of a farm in the Ozarks; of Fayetteville, Arkansas; a homestead in Saskatchewan; and even thought of buying Farm Island, in Farm Island Lake, just south of Aitkin, Minnesota. None of these would have proven practical, and what homesteads were left were, well, what were left.

Prairie Spring
oil on canvas, 30 x 36, c. 1950.

Waterfowl on migration were always an inspiration for Jaques. Here he paints great flocks of Richardson's Canada Geese passing north over Portage Creek, Manitoba.

The common thread through all these thoughts was to find a place close to wilderness and good hunting, and for this reason, the family decided to go north to Minnesota.

In the spring of 1903, the Jaques family packed what possessions they could into a spring wagon with hoops and a canvas top like a miniature prairie schooner. Their route took them from Kansas across Nebraska, part of South Dakota, and north through much of Minnesota.

> Alfred drove the team, Mother and Emma Jane just went along for the ride; while Father and I walked most of the way, which limited a day's travel to what we wanted to walk. The tent was pitched at night in the most attractive spot we could find, but frequently that was the roadside. Water might come from a farm, and for fuel, wood branches, if any, picked up along the way. This method of travel was conspicuous . . . for, while covered wagons were common enough, they were larger affairs and were going east or west — usually west — while we were heading north.

After six weeks of travel, they reached Aitkin. "This was late

Hooded Mergansers
watercolor, 20 x 16,
c. 1905.

In this early drawing, Jaques captures the essence of the riverine forests surrounding his home in Aitkin, Minnesota. The two small mergansers seem to be the only sparks of life in this otherwise cold, bleak scene of early spring.

spring or early summer and we were warned the road up the Mississippi River was not advised—too wet. Hardwood timber covered the immediate river region with bogs and muskeg inland. We went as far as we could go, seven miles north of Aitkin and bought a farm.

> Father called our place "Seven Oaks," and there were seven oaks in the field. . . . We cleared a garden and having only one spade took turns to keep the spade busy. Now spading a garden is a boring process, but there were birds, and I watched the birds and between heats drew birds. This may have been an unusual way to study birds, too.
>
> Wood ducks and Hooded Mergansers nested in our trees, Spotted and Solitary Sandpipers abundant. [In some] years Hawk Owls from the far north could be seen in the trees. Prairie Chickens sat in the trees every day in winter, so wild you couldn't get near them, and occasional Gyrfalcons from the far north. I saw several Swallow-tailed Kites, a bird [not seen] in Minnesota for over 50 years, and now being seen again.

Lee was now sixteen and his family led an isolated existence in their log cabin on an oxbow of the Mississippi River. His last schooling had been in a one-room farm school in Durham, Kansas, which he claimed did little to further his education. Fortunately, he liked to read and over the years developed an extensive education through many well chosen books. Most of his free time in Aitkin, however, was spent hunting, canoeing in the river, and, of course, drawing.

> Young artists ask me for advice, showing a dozen drawings they have done in the last year; this is like trying to become a pianist by practicing once every two months. When I was young, I drew constantly, though I had no idea I might ever do this as an occupation (Florence Page Jaques, *Artist of the Wilderness World*, p. 13).

To live on the land in northern Minnesota at the turn of the century, cutting trees for one purpose or another was essential. Lee and his father were often busy cutting timber, hauling and rafting logs, and chopping cord wood.

> Aitkin was an outfitting point for the woods—logging was almost entirely a winter occupation in northern Minnesota, depending on whether the swamps were frozen. A heavy early snow could prevent freezing and delay lumbering for weeks. From Aitkin the four-horse teams and sleds hauled supplies to the lumber camps farther north.
>
> At this period, great areas of dead tamaracks 6 inches or 8 inches in diameter stood in the swamps; they had been killed by a disease, but we didn't know that for many years. People just accepted tamaracks as dead and cut them, with an ax, into cordwood. They were too full of pitch to cut with a saw. Cordwood, of whatever species, was piled in great ricks in abundance. It was the only fuel and it takes a lot of wood to keep warm. To keep warm in winter, cutting, hauling, splitting and carrying wood into the house takes about half of one's time.
>
> Father, to be sure to get a contract, put in a bid to supply wood for the Court House in Aitkin for $2 a cord. The bid was ignored and Father made a fuss. The explanation was they'd found my drawings on the back of the bid and stuck it on the window, bid-side to the glass [and never saw the bid].
>
> Since it was a lower bid, they couldn't ignore it, and we did, Father and I, cut cordwood and haul it 7 miles for $2 per cord—on which you don't, by any means, get rich.

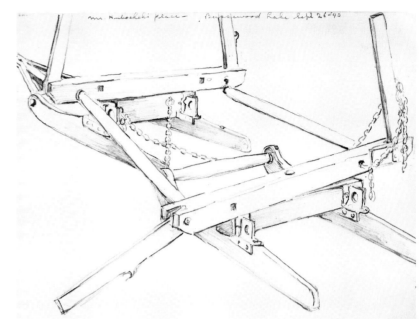

Logging Sled
pencil sketch, 8 x 9½, 1942.

Sketched in 1942 when Lee and Florence Jaques spent a winter in the Boundary Waters Area of northern Minnesota, this logging sled and barrel stove were much the same as those used during Lee's youth in Aitkin.

Wood Stove
pencil sketch, 17½ x 12, 1942.

Illustration for *Snowshoe Country*, by Florence Page Jaques.

As another source of income, they cut trees for timber and floated the logs down the Mississippi to the saw mills.

> Tools for the cutting and rafting were the ax and wedges, the peavy (a tool with a hook on it for rolling logs), and a pike pole – a long pole with a twisted pike on the end which you could jab into a floating log and lead it about.
>
> The logs were piled on the river bank so they could later be rolled into the river and made into a raft. There were three mills in Aitkin, down river, which processed hardwoods. I think we got $10 or so for a thousand board feet of basswood, except that the state scalers were corrupt. There were stumps of some gigantic white oaks on the land, but other than that none of the timber, elm, soft maple, basswood, or ash had been cut, so we cut it. Oak we saved for fence posts.
>
> In 1906, probably, I hewed railway ties all winter. They would buy ties made of almost anything then, though the price [they paid us] was low. To hew ties you flattened the sides of a log with a huge ax with a slightly bent handle and a 12-inch blade. You stood on the log and just before the ax fell, you removed the foot that stuck out over the side. When the tree was flattened to tie thickness, you cut it into tie lengths and hauled them to town.

One of the characteristics of Jaques's art throughout his career was his unsurpassed ability to portray trees. "After you have taken enough trees apart you know something about them and I know of no better way to learn to draw trees."

Lee studied game animals, too, for details of structure, color, and texture. However, he was most interested in the beauty of a bird's or mammal's form and movement. To learn to preserve the postures of living animals, Lee turned to taxidermy. He found a book on the subject and studied it intently. After doing some work on his own, he became an assistant to John Harrington, a taxidermist in Aitkin.

> John didn't have a very good idea of what a deer's head looked like. How he ever got interested in taxidermy is not clear. I improved his work some, but was frequently "corrected."

After one year, John moved to Duluth and Lee bought his business in the dilapidated shop for $10 in back pay.

From 1907 to 1916 Lee operated his taxidermy business during the winters, mounting mostly deer heads for six or seven dollars each.

> Those years were lonesome ones for me, especially evenings. I could hear footsteps creaking down the icy sidewalks.

He hoped that they would pause at his shop, and some did. But usually the footsteps receded, and he would remain alone.

> On a very cold, clear, still morning, while I was building up the fire in the front room, at dawn, I could see the tall, thin columns of wood smoke from every chimney and it was beautiful.
>
> Possibly, when one is depressed, visual beauty is more impressive, more poignant.

Lee had a few friends in Aitkin, and he was very much in love with a local girl, but the love was unrequited and only increased his isolation. He was a "lone wolf" and took long, solitary walks out into the country, often along railroad tracks.

> On a clear still night in winter, somebody's dog might bark, then a coyote

Dead Norway Pine
pencil sketch,
1943.

Jaques was an avid sketcher of trees. He felt that photographs of trees could never suffice as a reference, since their three-dimensionality was lost. His intent was to emphasize the way the branches had grown and been twisted by the wind. Only by studying and sketching the tree itself could he accurately convey a sense of the space and air around the branches.

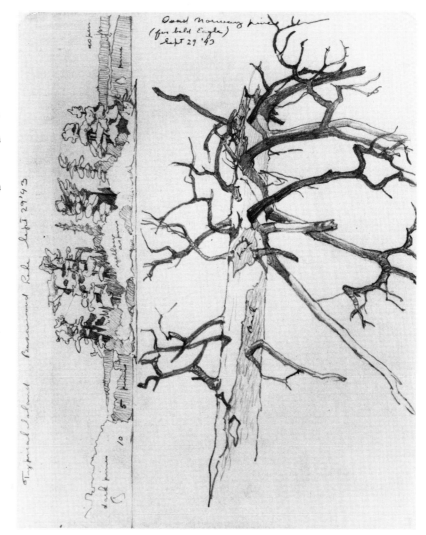

12

The Wolf Pack
oil on canvas, 30 x 36,
1945: courtesy of Dr. and
Mrs. Donald Duncan.

This image of a wolf pack at
full speed was reconstructed
from the pattern of tracks
Jaques followed along the
shore of a frozen northern
Minnesota lake. He had
known the cries and trails of
wolves from his early years
in Aitkin and strongly ad-
vocated the preservation of
this splendid wild creature.

or coyotes would cut loose and the timber wolves would come in with a chorus.

One snowy night while watching a train and the light from the firebox illuminating the sky, I suddenly thought "that's what I want to do – why not? Be a railroad man, fire locomotives." So that spring, 1913, I went down to Proctor and got a railroad job.

Railroading was not considered respectable work, and at the time, seemed like a great defeat for Lee. But it eventually freed him from Aitkin and led to a new life. It was a release like the coming of spring after a hard northern winter.

After a long, bitter winter on the farm near Aitkin or the taxidermy shop, the first signs of spring were very thrilling ideed. Cinders around the railway tracks increased the thaw, and bared bits of earth. I got a great pleasure from these early promises. On the farm, the first signs would be along the cut banks of the river, and later when the ice was thin, tiny holes of open water could be seen. Deep water, moving.

From 1913 to 1916, Lee worked during the summer as a fireman for the Duluth, Missabe, and Northern Railway and later for the Duluth and Iron Range Railway, returning the first few winters to work in his taxidermy shop. These railroads serviced the iron mines of northern Minnesota, bringing the ore to Duluth to be shipped down the Great Lakes. Lee had been fascinated with trains as a child when he watched them go by on the Rock Island Line behind his house in Geneseo. He also built his own toy trains, carving them from wood with wheels that turned, and one even had siderods that worked. Now for the first time, he was able to work with real engines.

> Hell, when I crawled up on that gigantic machine, with that great boilerhead before me, covered with the then modern filigree, with a grate surface about large enough for a square dance floor, I was scared. I think the engineman, faced with a green fireman, was scared too.

Railroading at that time was grueling work. Lee stoked some of the largest hand-fired engines ever built. For hours on end, he shoveled coal into the boiler, sometimes 12 to 15 tons a day. He became a member of the Brotherhood of Locomotive Firemen and Enginemen, but eventually realized that railroading did not hold much of a future for him. In 1916, he enrolled in a course in electrical engineering and took a job with the Great Northern

Mink in Snow
oil on canvas, 24 x 30, c. 1950: courtesy of Mrs. Helen Belford.

Jaques's paintings often reveal a sensitivity to the effects of climate and the subtle signs of changing seasons.

Cold Morning, Duluth
Railyard
oil on canvas, 36 x 30,
1930s: St. Louis County
Historical Society, Duluth,
Mn.

From his early days as a
locomotive fireman, Jaques
maintained a passion for
railroads, and despite his
love for wilderness, he was
still sensitive to the power
and beauty of this industry.

Power Company in Duluth. Nevertheless, trains remained a
lifelong interest. In later years he took many trips on both
modern and antique railroads throughout the world. He also extended his childhood toy-making to the development of an
elaborate and very personal miniature railroad layout he called
the "Great North Road," which is now displayed at the Lake
Superior Museum of Transportation in Duluth.

Even as he nursed along the great electrical generators at the
power company substation, he would watch, with fascination,
the trains nearby.

The great cathedral windows of the substation faced the Northern

Pacific round house, and all the trains into Duluth passed under the windows. In winter the smoke and steam in the frosty air was tremendous,
and I had, quite literally, nothing to do but watch. The windows got very
dirty so one night I drew pictures all over them with a finger, in the dirt.
This attracted much interest from the offices. The windows were
cleaned.

Lee's railroading experience also introduced him to the canoe
country along Minnesota's northern border.

> In the summer of 1913 I was firing locomotives on the D.&I.R. railroad
> and one afternoon, we made a trip from Ely to the Section 30 Mine. This
> was through a country so beautiful – it was one of those times or events
> which change the rest of your life and you know it.

As a result of that trip, he bought himself an eighteen-foot Old
Town canoe and for years explored this area of lakes, granite
shores, and pine forests.

> During these years there were several canoe trips, mostly with Tom
> Cassidy, who made the only good, or at least the best, canoe country
> maps. This was before the country had been surveyed and the portages
> were located by old fur-trader maps, in part. In a way, I suspect they
> were more accurate than present maps, except the shape of the lakes was
> only a guess, and we improved a lot of them just by looking.

In December 1917, after working less than a year for the power
company, Lee was drafted into the service for the First World
War. His unit was sent to San Francisco and trained at the
Presidio for coastal artillery duty. Despite the frustrations of
army life, Lee enjoyed his stay on the West Coast. He marveled at
the redwoods and eucalyptus trees, rode the train on Mount
Tamalpais and visited an exceptional art exhibition at the Palace
of Fine Arts. While installing an artillery gun emplacement in
Golden Gate Park, Lee discovered the California Academy of
Sciences. He had never visited a natural history museum before,
and the Academy had just opened a new hall of wildlife dioramas.

> One of the exhibits, a mule deer in a snowy forest, is to me about the
> finest exhibit of all time. It is still there. When I am in San Francisco, I
> go to the museum and sit in front of it and marvel.

Later, his unit was sent by train to New York, and during the ride
across the Rockies, Lee stood a double watch so that he could take
in the mountain scenery. His layover in New York was short, but
he recalls visiting several art museums before departing on a
cramped troop ship for England. After crossing the channel to
France, his unit was stationed in St. Emilion, far from the front,
where they waited for guns that never arrived.

After Armistice was declared in 1918, Lee returned to Duluth
and went to the power company to get his job back. He was offered the same pay he had started with two years earlier, so like
many other disappointed veterans, he went to the shipyards for
work. Here again he labored under extremely difficult conditions. He had to do the wiring work mostly while crawling on his
hands and knees in tight spaces. The steel ships were suffocating-
ly hot in the summer and numbingly cold in the winter. Eventually, a group of friends convinced him to put his artistic skill to

Return of the Voyageur, Picture Rock at Crooked Lake
oil on canvas, 49 x 40, early 1940s: courtesy of the Minnesota Historical Society.

For over a hundred years, the lakes and rivers along Minnesota's Canadian border formed the major fur trading route from Lake Superior to Winnipeg. Today, much of this area is protected by the Boundary Waters Canoe Area and Voyageurs National Park.

work and found him a job as a commercial artist at the Duluth Photo-Engraving Company.

> Our work in the P.E. was labels: toilet paper, match boxes, lettering of all kinds, drawing, dozens of drawings of useless devices to make a Model T Ford run better or to hold it together.

In Duluth, Lee took informal art lessons from his friend Clarence Rosenkranz, who taught Lee to blend oil colors, to define an object's characteristics, and to use light and shade to establish the illusion of three-dimensionality.

> His help was far greater and more useful to me than all other sources combined.

As a commercial artist, Lee was developing his innate ability to draw, but his subject matter was less than inspiring. He continued to spend his free time hunting and canoeing and working on paintings of his real love, wildlife and the wilderness. In the back of his mind, he held the memory of the mule deer exhibit in San Francisco and realized he wanted to be a museum artist.

Lee, however, was unknown in the museum world. When he made a hesitant inquiry of the Museum of Natural History on the

University of Minnesota campus, he received a discouraging reply. Carrying his disappointment, Lee returned to Aitkin and
took solace in duck hunting on Rice Lake.

> I had pulled my boat near shore, facing the lake while eating my lunch.
> While [I was] getting into the other end of the stuck boat to back off the
> shore, a Black Duck flew up, from literally only 4 or 5 feet away, where it
> had been hiding. It flew back over the land and I shot it.
>
> The ice had pushed up a ridge of muck, over the years, and tall grass
> grew on this ridge as well as on the flat land behind into which the duck
> fell. Because of the ridge I couldn't see where it fell, so I walked in and
> hunted a long time, in the tall grass, until I found it. I was just hunting
> for a duck. It is just possible that finding that duck changed the rest of
> my life.

Inspired by its beauty and flight, Lee did a painting of the black
duck. He sent this painting with two others to Dr. Frank Chapman at the American Museum of Natural History in New York.
Dr. Chapman, one of the leading ornithologists of the time, was
impressed by the painting, especially because this unknown and
untrained artist had correctly observed and painted the reversed
wing coverts of the duck. He showed the painting to others at the
Museum, and they convinced him to add Lee to the staff.

So, in 1924 at age 37, Lee Jaques left Minnesota for New York
City to embark on his new career. As his train approached New
York, it passed another train of 75 cars of watermelons.

> It rather impressed me. Must be quite a city that could eat a trainload of
> watermelons.

Black Duck Stamp
stone lithograph, 9 x 12,
1940.

Jaques was selected to design
the 1940 Federal Migrating
Waterfowl Stamp. He chose
a pair of Black Ducks as a
subject and displayed his
mastery at portraying birds
in flight with this design,
now a wildlife classic.

Still very much a "green country boy," Lee was appalled by the size of the city.

> The edge of the heavily inhabited area was what interested me. I wanted to know if the area *had* an edge. A series of trolleys took me to Patterson, New Jersey, from where I could walk up an escarpment and find land with no people on it. I felt better. There was an edge to the city.

Lee joined the American Museum as it was embarking on a program to renovate and expand the exhibits. Their old displays, like those of most natural history museums of the day, consisted mainly of dismal and poorly lighted glass cases filled with specimens of interest primarily to the experts. Lee recalled taking a tour of the museum and finding visitors using flashlights to read labels. However, in the 1920s, the conservation movement was growing. The museum was a center for this effort to preserve America's natural heritage and promote a better understanding and appreciation of the natural world. As growing industrialization and urbanization transformed society, new ways were needed to bring natural history to the city dwellers.

To revitalize its exhibits, the American Museum was developing new halls of habitat groups or dioramas. These dioramas were an attempt to recreate a natural location as accurately and beautifully as possible. A large landscape painting was done on a curved background wall, and this was merged with a full-sized reconstruction of the foreground scene. The rocks, plants, and

The End of the Line
oil on canvas, 30 x 36, ca. 1935.

In this painting of Canada Geese, Canvasbacks, and scaups on the New Jersey tidal flats, Lee combined his two great interests: waterfowl and railroads. During his years in New York City, he would often make short outings to backwater areas on the edge of the city and, whenever possible, combined bird-watching with train watching.

animals characteristic of the exhibit's locale or habitat were included in these groups. The museum's aim was to provide its visitors in New York City the opportunity to view slices of nature from throughout the world.

Dr. Chapman was active in this movement to popularize natural history. He edited *Bird Lore*, the forerunner of the *Audubon Magazine*, and often brought famous people down to see what Lee, "his man," was doing. Lee was thus swept into a world of dedicated artists and naturalists, and his talents blossomed.

> I think the period of about 1925 had more spirit, more promise than anything before or since and I was lucky indeed to be there at that time.

One of Lee's first projects was the dome of the main bird hall. He painted the dome as a great sky with many different species of waterfowl flying overhead. Mounted birds were suspended on piano wires so that they appeared to be flying across the sky. Dr. Chapman wanted the dome completed in time for the Annual Meeting of the American Ornithologists Union. Lee worked feverishly, finishing in less time than the regular painters had taken to prepare the surface. Roger Tory Peterson, then a teenager attending his first A.O.U. meeting, recalls walking into the hall and being compelled to look up, ignoring old-fashioned exhibit cases that lined the walls. Peterson asked the then unknown Jaques whether Bruce Horsfall, another artist had painted the dome. Jaques replied that he himself had done it. Later Peterson chastized himself for not having taken better advantage of his first chance meeting with Jaques.

When Lee first arrived at the Museum, his expertise was limited to the waterfowl he knew so well in Kansas and Minnesota, but his experience was soon expanded. As part of the process of creating museum habitat exhibits, Lee made many trips into the field. He observed and studied first-hand the wildlife and natural environments in many parts of the world. On these expeditions, he collected specimens and made field sketches of plants, animals, and other features of the chosen site. These were later used in constructing the exhibits back at the Museum. Lee's first excursion was to the tropical forests of Panama, a startling contrast to his familiar forests and prairies of the north.

> This was for source material for the first exhibit (groups we called them) for the new Birds of the World Hall. The subject, Tropical Rain Forest. The site was on Barro Colorado where there was a research station with buildings and equipment.
>
> Barro Colorado was a hilltop jungle which was left an island when Gatun Lake filled during the construction of the Panama Canal . . . the island had a good distribution of the typical birds and mammals of the wet tropics. It was there I saw a brown monkey hang by its tail and scratch itself with *all four legs at once.*
>
> The main tree of our exhibit was to be one we selected, a strangler fig, which is a sort of vine which weaves itself around a host tree, gets its leaves into the sunlight, grows, and eventually becomes a tree and strangles the host.
>
> Our host tree was a palm, about 8" through. If all parts of the cross section of the fig were in one round section, it might have been 20" in

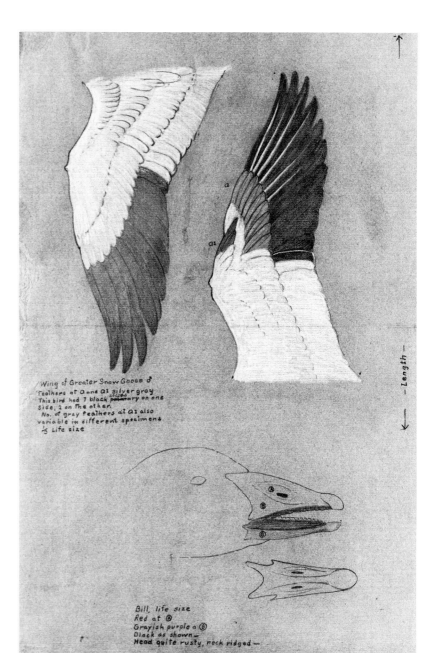

Wing of Greater Snow Goose ♂
Feathers at a and a1 silver gray
This bird had 1 black primary on one
side, 2 on the other.
No. of gray feathers at a1 also
variable in different specimens
½ Life size

Bill, life size
Red at ⓐ
Grayish purple a ⓑ
Black as shown —
Head quite rusty, neck ridged —

**Greater Snow Goose
Study**
pastel, 17 x 10,
c. 1925.

Jaques made many drawings
such as this to study the
anatomical structure of the
birds and other animals he
painted.

diameter, with a buttress and long roots above ground, reaching out. We
needed about 12 feet of this trunk. First we cut the palm above 12 feet,
and that fell. Then we carefully cut the radial roots of the strangler fig,
when we got all the roots off, and safe (all this had to be crated and
shipped back to the Museum) the fig wouldn't fall — its top being en-
tangled in the vegetation over head.

Dr. Chapman, who was offering little suggestions of no value, had ex-
plained to us that he wasn't allowed to do any work, presumably on the
advice of his doctor.

There was a big dead tree. I suggested we fell this into the mess and
everything would come down. "Oh no," said the Doctor. "Let's not
destroy the forest (the big tree would have rotted in a year); let's find
another one."

Well, Potter and I had perhaps two hard days' work each in the humid
tropics invested in that tree — and it was a good one — and we needed only
the bottom 12 feet.

I slept on the problem—that's a figure of speech; I probably didn't sleep much, but I worked out a way.

We cut two braces and notched them into the tree above the 12 foot mark, making a triangle, then got up and cut the fig above the props until it settled onto the props.

Obviously then, if we cut one prop, *something* had to happen and it did. We cut one prop and ran like hell.

The worst was yet to come. This had to be wrapped in burlap and carried to the dock but we had [the help of] some men, Indians, in this case and Doctor did his best to hurry us along not helping any. When the job was done [we] gave ourselves a couple of days vacation.

Strangler Fig Tree
pencil sketch, 18 x 12,
1925.

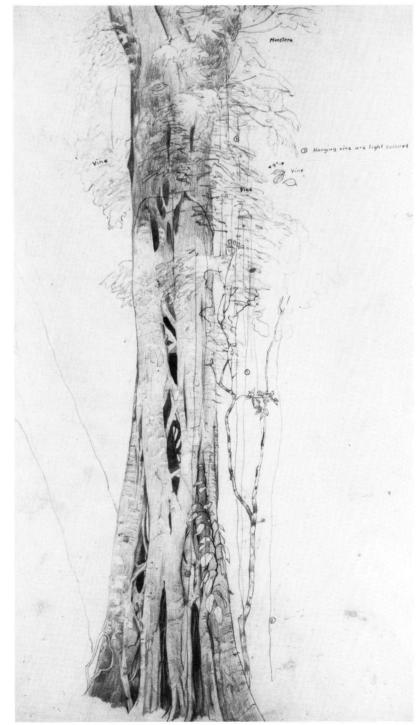

Piqueros, or Peruvian Boobies, Pescadores Island, Peru
oil on canvas, 29 x 38, c. 1935: illustration for Robert Cushman Murphy's *Oceanic Birds of South America,* courtesy of the Peabody Museum, Yale University.

In the 1920s Murphy served as an adviser to the Peruvian government on the conservation of their sea bird colonies, and investigated the natural cycles that supported them.

While in Panama, Lee was chosen to illustrate Robert Cushman Murphy's prospective book *Oceanic Birds of South America.* Since he was now more than halfway to Peru, he was sent on alone to gather source material.

> That required an emergency passport, money, which I carefully wasn't given much of, and "instructions."
> The coast of Peru is utterly barren almost all of the time. Murphy worked out a seven year cycle, when the sea water was warm and when there were rains. (This cycle has proved to be very unreliable.) The rains are a tragic time for Peru. Buildings are made of sun-dried mud and the rains don't help. What farming and vegetation there is, is due to irrigation, and the greenery is dusty.

In contrast to the desolate coast, the waters just offshore teemed with life. A combination of winds and currents bring cold, mineral-rich sea water to the surface. Marine life flourishes, including schools of anchovies by the trillions. The sea birds feed on these fish and nest in vast colonies on the rocky islands along the coast, where their droppings form thick deposits of nitrogen-rich guano. For years, the guano had been mined for fertilizer with complete disregard for the birds that produced it. To correct past mistakes, the Peruvian government established a Guano Administration to oversee the mining and protect the bird colonies. Nevertheless, natural catastrophes sometimes occur, when changes in the weather and currents bring rain to the coast, warm water to the shore, and the disappearance of the anchovies.

> Some months before my trip there had been rains, and almost all of the sea birds had died. I saw a little rain the first morning at Lima — *very* rare.

**Red-footed Cormorants
and Inca Terns**
oil on canvas, 38 x 29,
1935: illustration from
Robert Cushman Murphy's
*Oceanic Birds of South
America,* courtesy of the
Peabody Museum, Yale
University.

There were windrows of dried dead birds thrown up all along the coast, perhaps a thousand miles in extent.

After a stay in Lima, Lee went to the Chinchas Islands off Pisco. There were very few birds, so he went farther south to Independence Bay and the islands of Santa Rosa and Santa Rosita. The Guano Company wardens helped Lee as much as possible with his work, but communication was minimal.

I could speak no Spanish, they no English, but having read Murphy's book, and knowing what to expect, we got along fine – if I wanted to ask about a bird I drew a picture of it. No trouble!

Birds were scarce by normal standards – but there were plenty for my purposes. What were abundant were feather flies, about 5/8 inch long, 3/8 inch wide and not thick at all. They would crawl into the feathers of a bird and disappear, then out again giving a weird picture of the discomfort the birds suffered. There were so many feather flies on the Island they blew across and formed big drifts on the lee side. I made a crude easel and stretched a canvas, but it didn't work. The wind vibrated the canvas and the feather flies stuck to the paint. Other methods were in order. Photos and pencil sketches.

The most common birds were the Guanay Cormorant, the Peruvian Pelican, the Piquero, or Peruvian Booby, and several

Sea Lions
scratchboard, 6 x 7½.

From Victor von Hagen's
South American Zoo.

species of gulls. Inca Terns lived in caves cut by the waves and there were many Turkey Vultures. Sea lions were present on the outer rocks, but the wardens didn't permit them on the island proper.

> With one of the men we walked to the sea edge of the island and there, some 25 feet below us, asleep, was a gigantic bull sea lion. We threw stones at him, and he might have thought they were flies. If he thought at all. We climbed down thinking he must have been injured in the surf. I walked up and kicked him in the behind, no reaction whatever. Then we walked around in front of him and as soon as he opened one eye, he went plunging out through the surf in a series of sea lion leaps. Anyway, I've kicked a bull sea lion in the fanny.

Lee was greatly impressed by the coast of Peru. The tremendous surf caused by swells that were built up by westerly winds thousands of miles away in the South Pacific fascinated him, as did the great contrasts of this bare and rocky land.

> Looking shoreward across Independencia Bay, miles away with the glasses, was a great gentle slope of gravel. Nothing has ever grown there, nothing ever lived there, and across the whole mountain side is a crisscross pattern of lovely tracks. Whose tracks? Why? How many years have been recorded there? Nothing has ever left me so mystified, they seemed so small in time and space. I was grateful I knew something of this coast before I came. Nowhere on earth is there anything to equal it. Nowhere else is life so abundant and death so obvious.

Lee returned to Lima and then, despite a bad case of dysentery, went on to explore the coast and islands to the north. Andean Condors were common, and at one point he had eight in the field of his binoculars.

When Lee returned to the American Museum the first person he met said, "Haven't seen you around, been away?" Indeed, he was soon off again—this time to the Bahamas to paint tropical fishes and to obtain the terrestrial background material for the

Andean Condor
oil on canvas, 30 x 36,
1942; courtesy of Dr. and
Mrs. Robert Merrick.

Shortly before Jaques's first
trip to the Peruvian coast,
millions of birds had died
and washed up along the
shore. Many condors, gigantic birds with wing spans of
ten feet, had come down
from the Andes to feed on
the carcasses.

coral reef group, the main exhibit in the Hall of Ocean Life. The
painting of fish was new to Lee. Color studies had to be done
from living fish because their colors fade rapidly after death. As
Lee discovered, this problem is complicated in the case of
tropical reef fish.

> I had only a round glass bowl to put them in and fish take on a peculiar
> shape when seen through the sides of a glass bowl. And they change col-
> or or pattern or both at will. You start with one pattern and the fish goes
> through a complete change before you finish. Shake the
> bowl—sometimes he may go back to the original color.

Before returning, the expedition weathered a hurricane in their
rather unseaworthy yacht, the *Seminole.*

> The wind was high and that was the most terrifying boating experience I
> ever [had]. We had been anchored for some time with two anchors and a
> heavy line, and had swung around so the chains were twisted, making it
> almost impossible to hoist the anchors. We had finally to cut the line,
> and retreat with the *Seminole* to a small open bay inland on one of the
> channels. . . .
>   The anchors held and the *Seminole* stayed afloat. There wasn't
> anything one could do, but look at, and endure each other. One can't
> possibly get as wet outside [during] a hurricane as inside; just a super
> humid, reeking wetness which the walls can't stop, but it ended even-
> tually.

After the storm they finished their work and then returned over the Great Bahama Banks to Miami. "The water over the banks was a rich milky green, due to its being disturbed by the hurricane. White birds flying became a rich green against the blue sky due to reflected light."

Shortly before leaving for Peru, Jaques had moved into a new apartment in New York City. He couldn't afford much on his modest museum salary and he had looked long and hard before finding a room in the apartment of a pleasant older couple, the Galloways. The room looked out over the Hudson River to the Palisades in New Jersey and beneath it was Riverside Drive and the tracks of the New York Central freight lines. On his return, he discovered that there was some competition for this room. A Miss Florence Page, a friend of the Galloways who had formerly rented the room, now wanted it back. Lee, however, liked the room and, having paid rent on it for the months he was away, did not want to give it up. So Florence took another room, closer to Columbia University, where she was attending poetry and story writing classes.

Florence often came to see the Galloways and often would see Lee. Florence was well educated, sociable, and articulate; she had led a fairly sheltered life, drawing her knowledge of the world mostly from books. Lee, on the other hand, was shy, quiet and educated largely by direct experience. Initially, he was not particularly impressed by Florence. "This Miss Page hadn't done very much except lie in a hammock and read." However, since they each had rooms without cooking facilities, they began joining each other for dinner. "We both had to eat out somewhere, so why not eat together?" They also started to go to the theater and museums and on trips into the country together. As it turned out, they both were interested in nature and loved the out-of-doors. Lee recalls that, "for the first time in my life the pieces were fitting together, beautifully."

Florence softened the hard edges of Lee's serious, work-oriented personality. She taught him to play, to laugh at himself a little, and helped him enjoy the company of others. Lee added intensity and focus to Florence's life. Together, they were soon off on all sorts of outdoor adventures, usually involving birds in one way or another. They were married in 1927.

> This was the great turning point, life from here on was infinitely better. We've never had any trouble about women or money and lived happily ever after.

They took their honeymoon in the fall, when they made their first canoe trip together into the Quetico-Superior wilderness on the border between Minnesota and Ontario.

Florence habitually kept a journal but now her trips with Lee gave her more to write about. After having several magazine articles published, she was asked by the University of Minnesota Press to expand her journal into a book illustrated with Lee's drawings. The book, *Canoe Country*, published in 1938, was a great success and has become a Minnesota classic. It was the first of a series of joint ventures in which Florence's poetic, light, and

Frigate Birds in the Bahamas
oil on canvas, 33 x 26, 1927-28; courtesy of Henrietta Page Johnson

Jaques loved the tropical seas with their rich patterns of sky and clouds, and the sharp color changes between deep water and shallow reefs.

humorous writing was beautifully complemented by Lee's unique and forceful scratchboards.

Less than a year after their marriage, Lee was offered the opportunity to join an expedition to Alaska and the Arctic Ocean on the Schooner *Effie M. Morrissey*. Lee had been fascinated by accounts of Arctic exploration and this trip was too good to miss, though he was hesitant to leave Florence. The schooner was in the charge of Captain Bob Bartlett, who had skippered Robert Peary's ship on the first successful attempt to reach the North Pole. He was a Newfoundlander, a colorful character, and one of

Canoeists in Rapids
scratchboard, 17 x 21, 1960; illustration for *The Lonely Land* by Sigurd F. Olson.

In September 1927, Lee Jaques returned to the border lakes of northern Minnesota for a canoe trip. This time he brought his new wife, Florence, who would later write of their experiences in *Canoe Country*.

the last sea captains to explore the Arctic in sailing vessels.

> Cap'n Bob would begin at meals, . . . and rib everybody around the table in turn—always good natured. Or tell us a story. Nobody said, "Cap'n, tell us a story," the stories were there, needing only time for telling.

Lee's task was to collect material for several exhibits planned for the American Museum. Other members from the Museum were Andy Johnson, preparator; Harold Anthony, Curator of Mammals; and Ed Weyer, archaeologist. Harold McCracken, who organized the expedition, and Charles Stoll, a real estate developer who financed it, were mostly interested in hunting big game.

> Mr. Stoll had stowed in with our supplies a large canvas with the gigantic letters, "Lots for Sale" painted on it. This was installed on an ice floe somewhere near Herald Island in the Arctic Ocean—and duly photographed.

The Museum crew planned to meet the *Morrissey* at Prince Rupert, British Columbia. They were to sail up the inside passage to Juneau, Alaska, then out across the Gulf of Alaska to the Aleutian Islands, eventually making their way through the Bering Strait to the Arctic Ocean. Contact with the *Morrissey* was maintained by amateur short-wave radio operators with messages sent to the New York Times. In May, 1928, they started up the inside passage.

> Many birds were seen, of species new to me. I was constantly on deck. The mountain scenery was beautiful.

After reaching Juneau, they headed for Stag Bay.

Stag Bay is a narrow, deep fjord on the north west corner of Chichagof Island, the upper slopes [were] deep in wet snow. Water would accumulate behind a mass of snow, which would give way and many tons of snow and water come tumbling down the mountain side. The effects of snowslides were evident in the forest. A rugged, astounding region, and since it was rarely visited, full of wildlife.

There were drumming Blue Grouse which I couldn't locate since the drumming sound can't be located. I later realized they were in the tops of trees, and safe from me.

This was tremendous country – deep moss – one couldn't tell whether there was something under the moss for support, or a deep hole. If you grabbed something for support it was devil's club, with [an] abundance of long thorns.

We left Stag Bay May 9th in a snowstorm, gigantic flakes as fitting this over-scale region, and saw hummingbirds flying across the inlets in the snow. Ravens were tumbling, turning upside down and running in flight.

The ship then entered the open ocean, the Gulf of Alaska, on its way to the Aleutian Islands.

Outside, in the Gulf of Alaska that evening, the top of Mt. Fairweather, clear in the sunset light, appeared above the haze, and I have mentally recorded it as one of the great moments of my life.

Suddenly we were at sea – a different world – with different birds. Sea birds predominated, large flocks of Sooty Shearwaters appeared, and Black-footed Albatross, Fork-tailed Petrels, [and] many Fulmars. This was soon one of my favorite birds, about, as a guess, 20 to 22 inches long with a big bill and head and big black trusting eyes and short stiff wings. They loved to come alongside the *Morrissey* and experience the bumpy air which spilled from the sails. Their flight was of necessity much faster than the speed of the *Morrissey* so they made great circles over the water and every few minutes would be back alongside. There was a wide variation in the plumage so one could know, personally, a large number of individual birds.

All the Tubinaries, or Tube-nosed Swimmers, albatrosses, shearwaters, fulmars . . . have their own rapid almost effortless flight, depending on winds and waves. . . . Behind even a moving wave there is some shelter, a little less wind. The birds come up against the wind behind the wave just over the water, their long narrow wings, set low on the body and curved downward, the tips of the wings sometimes touching the water – just. When the bird reaches the top of the wave it meets a fresh, higher speed gust of air, which it uses to shoot up into the air, gaining elevation. With this it slides off, gaining speed into another trough between the waves, where the same circuit begins over again. On numerous occasions I have seen an albatross and a fulmar, a much smaller bird, apparently one chasing the other, till I came to realize they were each following the same invisible best path through the air.

The expedition reached the Aleutians and stopped at Belkofski on May 17. They hoped to reach the Bering Sea through False Pass but it proved too difficult and dangerous for a ship with as little auxiliary power as the *Morrissey*. They then made for Urinak Pass which added several days of very rough weather to the voyage.

Well, finally into and through Urinak Pass, sharing it with many thousands of shearwaters on their way into Bering Sea for our summer. Imagine then a great many birds flying as described above. It results in a great rolling windrow of birds miles long – endless, as far as we could see – one of the great sights of the oceans, which we saw again near Bering Strait.

On May 22, they anchored at Moller Bay on the Alaskan Peninsula, one of the windiest bays in the world, with tidal currents that made controlling the ship very difficult.

The big game party left in the small boats for the head of Moller Bay, for bear. This was bear and caribou habitat – the bear . . . were to be for an exhibit in the Museum. Ed Weyer and myself had our own little camping expedition – Ed for Aleut artifacts and I to collect birds and get a background sketch for a possible bear group. From a high point I did a panoramic (three sheets of paper) sketch of the Mountains at the head of Moller Bay – a most astounding mountain range.

Ed and I established camp at the hot springs just south of Moller Bay. The water from this spring led through a series of small ponds in which the natives had arranged controls, so you could bathe in a pond with the exact water temperature you wished. The ground around the spring was warm, and what could be better? Excellent – wait. By the first morning our bedclothes – *all* our clothes – were more than a little damp. We could have moved camp, but in that climate, a day for drying bed clothes was very rare indeed!

The spring was fine for boiling eggs. Just put the eggs in the spring in the evening and they were just right in the morning. On the way over to the hot springs I had shot into a flock of phalaropes (very delicate shore birds) and picked up thirteen. Thirteen was more than I needed for skins, so we put *them* in the hot springs, and they were barely edible. We tried some gulls, and they just never softened up. They just had a layer of

Eiders Offshore
casein, 20 x 23, 1928.

This painting of King and Common Eiders was done on board the schooner *Morrissey* during the 1928 Stoll-McCracken Expedition to the Arctic. Near the Aleutian Islands, the *Morrissey* encountered thousands of sea birds on their migration north.

Moller Bay, Alaska
pencil sketch, 11 x 26,
1928.

In this panoramic pencil
sketch, Jaques records with
detailed notes the subtle colors of the surrounding tundra, and delineates the spectacular mountains of the
Alaskan peninsula.

sulphur or something outside. . . . I expect Ed, who is an excellent
story teller, is still telling of our culinary experiences at the hot springs.

The Alaskan Peninsula is treeless except that around Moller, there
were patches of Alders, rugged twisted bushes that might be 15' high and
impenetrable, wonderful places for bear hideouts. But you had to walk
around them, and at the lower elevations, to get from here to there—you
had to plan your route in advance. And at the lower levels, there was
much grass and an abundance of water—little streams were everywhere
and were often overgrown with moss and grass. Very hard walking until
one got to a higher elevation, when the walking got progressively better.
Looking across an expanse of this tundra there was a great tapestry of col-
or—purples and tans and greens and reds of many shades. To me a most
beautiful landscape—and always with the snow mountains in the
distance.

Andy and I spent the time from June 10th to 20th at King Salmon
Creek, in a native barabara, or semi log and sod house, the wood being
driftwood.

Ground squirrels were common, and were the big bear's favorite
food—the bear just tore up the ground until he came to the squirrel in his
burrow. We didn't see a bear, though bear "sign" was common. . . .
There was an abundance of nonbreeding gulls, and every few minutes an
eagle flew over a patch of gulls on a mud flat but the gulls just flew and
the eagle paid them no further attention. Had there been a sick gull, the
eagle would have caught it. I think they caught candle fish in the creek,
where the fish were "running." I shot a Harlequin Duck and had to wade
the creek to get it, moving my feet—bare feet—carefully forward through
the hoards of fish to avoid stepping on them. I don't like to step on fish!
The eagles liked to sit on the slightly higher bits of tundra, which
resulted in fertilizing that very small area so the growth was more
rank—you could easily spot an eagle's perch (the ground was all they had
to perch on) by the vegetation.

There was visible from King Salmon Creek a dirty mountain (the
painting "Swans over Tundra" was from this area). Whenever I came
back to the barabara I found Andy skinning a ground squirrel. I think
each time it was the same squirrel.

Eventually, the *Morrissey* left Moller Bay and returned to the
Aleutians in search of an island that was purported to have an-

Swans over Tundra
oil on canvas, 30 x 42,
1928.

Before Lee left for the Arctic, he and Florence took an early spring holiday to Chesapeake Bay. They were bird-watching in the salt marshes when a pair of Whistling Swans flew low overhead. Later, Lee glimpsed swans from the train in Saskatchewan on his way to the West Coast. In Alaska, while he was walking in the tundra, a pair again flew over, and he imagined they may have been the same Chesapeake swans at the end of their long migration.

cient Aleutian burial sites. The suspected island was small, turf covered, with sheer rock walls dropping to the sea. Only one cleft in the rock provided access to the top. Partway up this cleft, the landing party encountered human skeletons and artifacts confirming their belief that the island was a burial site. On the grassy top they found evidence of human activity as well as the burrows of nesting puffins. Partly exposed by these diggings was the corner of an underground wooden structure. The party dug through the turf, exposing a sarcophagus carefully constructed of driftwood, seal skins, and straw matting. It contained five partially mummified bodies and artifacts of stone, wood, and bone. The preservation was remarkable, but no metal or other indications of a recent age were found.

Lee had not joined this search and took a dim view of the proceedings.

> The island party returned from the first days adventures, saying little or nothing, but prepared to go again in the morning for a longer stay, taking supplies in larger than necessary boxes.
> They came back the same evening with some "mummies" in the boxes. . . . I suspect that these bodies just may have had rather recent [descendants] still living in the villages. The island party was ready to move on the next morning. Even eager.

They then headed north to the Bering Strait, some 600 miles away. As the *Morrissey* neared the strait, its propeller shaft broke, and they were in danger of being swept into the Arctic Ocean without power. Lowering the motorized whale boat and launch, the crew managed to push the disabled schooner to the Alaskan coast near Teller. There, after two weeks and much struggle, a new shaft was installed. The expedition was now well behind schedule and the short Arctic summer was passing rapidly.

On July 27, they left Teller en route to the Diomede Islands, two adjacent islands in the Bering Strait, one American and one Russian. Here at Little Diomede, Lee collected materials for an exhibit featuring the granite cliffs where thousands of kittiwakes, murres, puffins, and other birds nested. Landing near these colonies was impossible, so Lee took photographs and notes from the tossing launch just outside the breaking waves and rocks.

What had seemed from a distance dull and drab, now proved to be many-colored and beautiful. Rich green vegetation followed the rock slides down from the upper slopes toward the water's edge. At the base the slow rise and fall of the dark water was transformed to green and white where it met the opposing granite. Myriads of birds flew overhead and around the great walls or perched in long lines on ledges (Jaques, Francis Lee, "Birds of Little Diomede," *Natural History*, Sept.-Oct. 1929, p. 522).

Many birds had to be collected and skinned. One evening I was working below decks and heard what I thought was the surf, which puzzled me as we didn't seem to be rolling more than usual; then one of the men came down and said, 'You ought to come on deck and see the birds.' Which I did.

The air was full of auklets of three species. Auklets as far and as high as you could see, everywhere, going in every direction. They had come in from the sea and were climbing, . . . possibly a thousand feet to the top of the island, where their burrows were. The sound of their wings continued until nearly noon the next day.

Leaving the Diomedes, we headed for Herald Island, after walrus and polar bear. One evening, while I was on deck and the rest were playing poker below, I saw a walrus, the first walrus, . . . swimming parallel to the *Morrissey*—perhaps 100 yards away. All sea mammals prefer to swim underwater, coming up only to grasp a chunk of air when necessary. I called the others, and they reluctantly came on deck—and went down again before the walrus came up for air. After that, what I saw was mine.

We got within eight miles or so of Herald Island, but the ice was too heavy, and we couldn't make it. So the balance of our time was spent in the search for walrus, and material for the setting of the walrus group for the Hall of Ocean Life, in the Museum.

Ice floes are pretty well scattered over this part of the ocean north of the Diomedes in summer. There are no glaciers or icebergs, but pressure ridges form some large masses of ice. Pools of water on the floes are fresh, and furnish the fresh water supply.

Only four species of birds were seen at our farthest north. The Pomarine Jaeger, the Red Phalarope, and the Ivory Gull (off Herald Island), also Mandlt's Guillemots.

In calm weather, among the scattered ice it was hard to believe you weren't in inlets along the Jersey coast, with snow on the marshes. The bottom all through this area is down about 150 feet, and walrus feed on clams, which they swallow shell and all.

Enough walrus were killed for the exhibit. They were on the ice floes—and eventually hoisted aboard—skinned, and whatever. The deck of the *Morrissey*, thick with grease and blood, was a slippery, hazardous place. On a frosty morning, portions of walrus left all night were steaming, still hot.

Walrus are extremely ugly, cumbersome and awkward on land or ice, and individually very different. It would be easy to distinguish your walrus friends, if any.

For most of this time in the ice floes, Captain Bob Bartlett stayed in the lookout barrel on the foremast, guiding the ship by shouting down commands. They continued to search for polar bears, but the weather turned stormy, and the ice that was at first scattered became heavier and more closely packed. The Arctic summer was coming to a close and the Captain was becoming anxious. Having lost a ship to the crushing ice on an earlier voyage, Captain Bob decided to "get the hell out of here," and set a course southward. When the *Morrissey* reached the Bering Strait, it appeared blocked by newly frozen sea ice. Luckily, the ice was still soft and they steamed through it to the open sea to the South.

In Panama, Peru, and the Arctic and on other later expeditions, Lee's major concern was to prepare preliminary studies for the large mural paintings that would form the backgrounds for the habitat exhibits at the museum in New York. The usual field procedure was to select a location with the most dramatic scenery

Morrissey and Glaucous Gulls
oil on canvas,
1934; courtesy of Dr. Junius Bird.

As the Arctic summer was drawing to a close, the *Morrissey* threaded its way among the ice flows near Herald Island, in search of polar bears. Often the ship was enveloped in fog and mist, with the constant danger of being trapped by the ever-shifting ice.

Alps
pencil sketch, 23½ x 32,
1935.

Sketched at Zermatt,
Switzerland, for a diorama
exhibit at the American
Museum of Natural History
in New York, this simple
drawing clearly shows the
structure and contours of
the mountain peaks and
alpine meadows.

and do a small oil painting on the spot. A series of photographs also would be taken for later reference. In both Peru and the Arctic, Lee contended with conditions that prevented him from doing full landscape paintings in the field. On the Chinchas Islands the wind, heat and blowing feather flies combined to make oil painting impossible. In the Arctic the cold rains and tossing seas had the same effect. Photographs could still be taken and Lee took many, but this period was long before color film had been perfected.

To overcome these difficulties, Lee developed a system of field sketching to efficiently record essential information. He drew rapidly but with great precision; working from one sheet of his sketch pad to another, building a panoramic drawing of the scene. Sometimes his early drawings have a great deal of shading, but many, especially his later ones, such as the drawing of the Alps, have very little. Shading information is usually well recorded in black and white photographs and thus is not essential to draw in the field; however, the colors of the scene and the relative positions in space of the scene's various components can be understood only by observation in the field. Jaques's sketches thus tend to emphasize the contours and structure of the landscape and to delineate areas of color. Scattered throughout the drawings are color notations coded to a color chart. The finished sketch, which often has a paint-by-number appearance, is in reality a thorough analysis of the color and structure of the landscape. From these sketches and color charts, Lee was able to recreate the essence of the scene in the museum exhibit. This process of sketching a landscape by delineating areas of color and emphasizing contours and spacial relationships strongly influenced his finished painting style.

But Jaques's interests did not end with the background painting. Possibly because of his extensive experience with hunting and taxidermy, he was given responsibility for collecting the animals, plants, and other materials needed for the exhibit foreground. He hunted specimens, prepared skins, and took measurements that would be needed for the group construction. Although tasks such as skinning walrus and brown bears in the Arctic were not always pleasant, Jaques used these opportunities to study and draw whatever he was working on.

Some of his most charming and exacting studies are of tropical plants from Panama and rock formations from the Peruvian coast. The shapes, colors, and cross-sections of the tropical leaves are drawn, and nest locations are carefully marked on the rock faces, showing the intensity and thoroughness with which he observed and recorded nature. He had a philosophy about observation which he called the Jaques Law: "It is that one sees as much while walking, or one might also say, while sitting still, as one does at higher speeds. In other words, it is the time lapse that counts." He knew that what could be seen and known about nature was endless; the limiting factors were the time and intensity given by the observer.

Travel and exploration of new parts of the world was always a joy for Lee, and the more isolated the localities the better. In 1934, he was given the opportunity to join a six-month museum expedition to the South Pacific on board a sailing yacht, the *Zaca.*

> About 90 feet long, 83 net tons, the *Zaca* was built on the lines of the famous schooner *Blue Nose* but smaller. Speed, frequently 200 miles per day. Two motors.

The expedition left San Francisco in September to explore many isolated and, at that time, rarely visited islands. Lee was to collect materials for habitat groups in the Marquesas, in the Tuamotus, on the Peruvian coast, and in the Galapagos Islands. They also were to stop at Tahiti, Pitcairn, Easter, and many other islands.

> Contrary to the *Morrissey* cruise the *Zaca*'s trip was well planned—it was to be the perfect trip. There were no guests. Everybody was paid.
> Oil had been sent ahead to remote places. Food was frozen. We had a good cook. For me—too good. I should have preferred fresh fish (only the crew got fresh fish). What we as gentlemen got was from the Highest Sources—no expense barred.
> The time of year was selected to avoid storms, and we had pleasant weather throughout—never a storm.

The expedition's sponsor and owner of the *Zaca* was Templeton Crocker, inheritor of a financial and business empire in California.

> Crocker lived in a penthouse on top of Nob Hill, over his own apartment

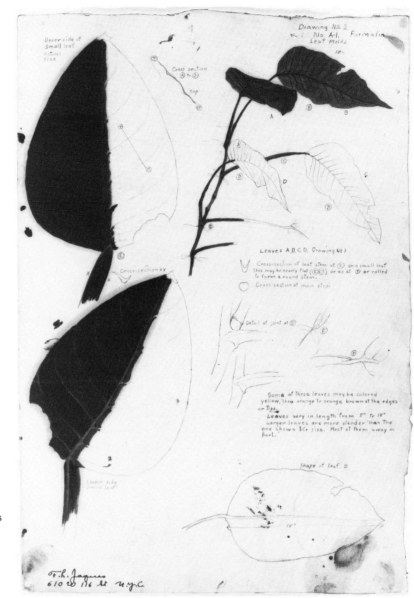

Tropical Plant Sketch
pencil and oil on paper,
12 x 17½,
1925.

Although Jaques often felt
that tropical vegetation was
too lush and "messy" for his
taste, he did many beautiful
and detailed studies of plants
on Barro Colorado Island,
Panama. The drawings were
later used to reconstruct
models of the vegetation for
exhibits at the American
Museum.

building. The four-sided all-glass room was lighted by crescent moons projecting from beneath the floor. The view from the room was magnificent. All the lights of San Francisco and the Harbor. Around the outside of the room were pools of water which were almost invisible. But we didn't fall in.

Crocker, however, was an eccentric, and throughout the voyage, kept everybody to absurdly rigid schedules, and seemed to go out of his way to create uncomfortable situations.

To put it bluntly, Crocker had, or got, a morbid pleasure from being miserable and if he could share that pleasure with others who had no escape hatch, that was good too.

The *Zaca* sailed on the precise minute at 6 P.M. romantically into the sunset out through the Golden Gate. The timing put us over the bar outside at dinner time, but nobody got seasick—not even Crocker.

The first evening I had a long friendly talk in the moonlight with Crocker and found he liked crossword puzzles. I said Florence liked puzzles too, doing those in the *New York Times*, and Commodore (which he called himself) Crocker gave me distinctly to understand he didn't stoop to the *N. Y. Times*, that he only did those from the *London Times*!

Meanwhile Florence, on her way home, was reading Crocker's book on his [earlier] 'round the world trip on the *Zaca* and was puzzled to note that Crocker's guests were leaving the ship at every port.

Fortunately, others shared on the voyage, and Lee got along well with the crew. The staff from the American Museum were Harry Shapiro, Curator of Anthropology, and James Chapin, who was famous for his studies of African birds. The person Lee liked best was Toshio Aseada, a Japanese-American employed by Crocker as a photographer on all his trips.

Having photographed nearly the entire Pacific Ocean, Toshio and [his] wife were interned for four years during the war. No one could have been more loyal, but they seem not to be bitter about it.

Toshio could do essentially *anything* useful to a museum. He collected material for several Whitney Hall groups and it was excellent. When we saw them last, Toshio, long past retirement age, was indispensable at the Academy of Sciences in San Francisco.

Their first stop was Nuka Hiva in the Marquesas. A high, volcanic island divided by sharp ridges into numerous valleys and bays, it is the setting of Herman Melville's novel *Typee*.

The exhibit was to be inland but we wanted a scenic background somehow related to where Herman Melville had been held captive by the natives. That required a trip to another bay. . . . Chapin and I walked up the valley then up the slope through the hibiscus forest to get on the ridge. It was hot and humid and I was ready to quit and was about to tell Jimmy to stop for me on his way back (he never could have re-traced his steps) but we continued and came out on top of a long treeless ridge facing down to the sea toward the southeast. These ridges are almost knife sharp and covered with bracken. The view was wonderful all around and gave a wonderful chance to follow Melville's trip across the island and explain his misfortune.

They also visited several other islands in the Marquesas including Hiva Oa where the artist Paul Gauguin spent his last days.

The local people told stories about him, how he drove around with horse and cart and how he was enough of an exhibitionist to be conspicuous to even South Sea Islanders.

While Lee and Chapin were studying birds and collecting material for exhibits, Harry Shapiro was busy interviewing the local people.

Harry Shapiro was interested in the sex life of the natives—whatever anthropologists are concerned about. He went from house to house of course, and the content of his questions spread far ahead of him and the gals had their answers ready far in advance.

Sailing south, they next stopped at the Hao islands in the Tuamotus, a group of low coral atolls.

Most large atolls, Hao especially, have an inlet—or better said, outlet. Some parts of the reef are always or almost always under water, and the surf wraps clear around the island throwing water to the inside resulting in a higher water level inside the lagoon. This results in a continuously flowing current—out. The current was so strong it wasn't easy to get in. A native pilot directed us, and since the *Zaca* was larger than most local

Taipee Valley, Nuka Hiva
Island, Marquesas,
oil on canvas, approx.
20 x 45,
1934; courtesy of the
American Museum of
Natural History.

After an arduous climb to
the top of this ridge, Jaques
knew he could not return
with painting equipment. Instead, he took photographs
and painted this three-part
panorama on board the *Zaca*
while the colors of the scene
were still fresh in his mind.

schooners he tended to want us too far to the side where we were watching the bottom through the clear water. Hard lumps of coral. The *Zaca*
touched bottom once, and Frank went overboard to inspect, and found
no trouble. He was so proud to be of use but Crocker wasn't satisfied and
hired a professional diver at Tahiti to investigate the bottom.

Some of these islands atolls had no channel to the lagoon. The
islanders come and go by paddling their outrigger canoes through
the surf and over the coral reef.

It is a hard life. Coral has cutting edges and the wounds don't heal prop-
erly, and the natives are disfigured – elephanti was common, and
glamour absent.

They spent Thanksgiving in Tahiti.

We were invited for dinner to Moorea, an island visible from Tahiti.
This is a breathtaking, mountainous cove. The guests came, singing and
strumming guitars, in Old Town canoes.
      The next stops were south of Tahiti, Rimetara, Rurutu, Raevavae and
Rapa in that order – all high islands with surrounding coral reefs.
      It was on one of these islands where I saw, to me, the most interesting
sight of the trip. We were floating outside the reef on a dark night, the
water being too deep to anchor. Seven outrigger canoes came over the
reef – each with many bundles of palm fronds – dry. A heavy swell was
running, but it wasn't windy – a bundle of fronds would be hung on a
pole on each canoe, forward, and these lighted. With this light natives
with long poles with nets on the ends were dipping flying fish out of the
air for food! I wish I could give a picture of this. The dark land, sensed,
but not really seen. The roar of the surf, more sensed than seen, and the
seven great fires with the attendant reflections, rising and falling in the
swell. These men, thinking not at all of art, were putting on a pretty
magnificent show of moving lights.

From Rapa they sailed to Mangareva. Lee found this island
remarkable for its open, high hills covered with bracken ferns.
On one hill stood a stone cathedral with stone roads leading to it
from all over the island

Missionaries are in evidence on all the islands – not one sect, but several
on each. There seems to be a great urge to tell someone else what to
think – and you'd better think it too, or you'll burn in Hell!

Jaques resting on Hao Island, Tuamotus; courtesy of the California Academy of Natural Sciences.

On December 23, they landed on Pitcairn Island, inhabited by descendants of the HMS *Bounty* mutineers and Polynesian women. As the *Zaca* lay at anchor in Bounty Bay, the crew spent Christmas and New Year's day on the Island.

Bounty Bay, Pitcairn Island, was very small indeed. Landing was entirely managed by the inhabitants in their own whale boat. They did not come out for us on the split second timing which Crocker preferred, within an hour was plenty soon enough. The landing required something like 20 minutes. They would row up to just outside the reef – rocks in this case and wait for the "seventh wave" – all pull hard on the oars and go over the reef, row rapidly across the "bay," only a couple of boat-lengths to the beach, jump out and pull the boat up out of the reach of the waves.

I went all over the island with altimeter and compass, and the Captain went around the island twice and Toshio took numbers of photographs. From it all I drew a much better contour map of Pitcairn than any of the charts we had.

The whale boats or home-made long boats of the Pitcairn Islanders carried 14 oars or men, one man per oar – and perhaps twice that many people. There were two of the boats, and they once put on a race for us.

After bringing us aboard in the evening they, too, would come aboard, disturbing the alcoholic schedule until the Commodore could get them into the long boat again. Then they would lay alongside in the swell and sing hymns to us, once in the rain. One of the hymns I remember was "Shall we gather at the river?" Particularly touching, because none of them had ever seen a river.

Just before leaving, the islanders invited the entire *Zaca* crew to a New Year's dinner of wild goat shot on the hills of the island. As Lee reminisced,

Leavetaking is poignant in Polynesia – they ask, "are you going to your island?" – never having known anything but island life.

From Pitcairn, the expedition headed east, stopping briefly at the small uninhabited island of Ducie, with its colonies of nesting tropic birds and boobies, and then on to Easter Island.

Easter was a grass island devoted to raising sheep. A ship (in '35) came out once a year. Most visitors were from cruises and expeditions, like us.

The great stone images (with hats so big that broken, leftover hats at the point marked 'Hat quarry' were large enough so cattle sought their shade) were originally standing on great stone platforms at intervals all around the island, with their back toward the sea. All of these were pushed over and broken by later explorers. They are of such soft stone – lava – that the stone crumbled [in] the hand.

Leaving Easter Island, the *Zaca* continued heading toward the Chilean coast.

Between Easter and Chile is an enormous permanent high pressure area without storms. The air is crystal clear. Five mile high clouds, normally visible only when silhouetted against the sunset are visible all day with only the *tops* showing over the horizon. A long hardly perceptible swell runs from the "roaring forties" to the coast of South America. The title for the painting *Zaca* is quoted from the Captain's noon log on one of these days: "Sea – smooth long lazy southwesterly swell." The distance from Easter to Chile is about as far as from New York City to Ireland – the swells can run free twice that distance. I felt, thought then [that] nothing that man has done can change the position of one wave, or alter the plans of flying fish. . . . That is no longer true.

Pitcairn Island
oil sketch, 12 x 9, 1934; courtesy of Thomas Young.

As well as doing this small landscape painting, Jaques walked all over Pitcairn with an altimeter and compass, making a more accurate map of this tiny, isolated island than any of the charts the expedition had.

On the way to Valparaiso, Chile, the *Zaca* stopped briefly at two islands, Mas Afuera and Juan Fernandez.

Mas Afuera is a grass covered cone, with deep eroded gullies at intervals.

A species of petrel nested on the island, but in the daytime they are in burrows, and we hadn't got any. As we were leaving at dusk, the petrels began to come in from the sea. We were all aboard ship and Chapin and I

The Zaca and Tropic Bird
oil on canvas, 30 x 24, 1962; courtesy of Geneste Anderson.

Between Easter Island and the coast of Chile, the *Zaca* passed through an area of nearly permanent calm. Here the great ocean swells used by the Pacific Islanders for navigation could be easily felt.

tried to collect some for the museum. We both missed 5 or 6 shots each.

Crocker, being owner, elbowed himself to go forward and from his better position killed one. Captain was at the wheel, he came about hard to go back and pick up the birds and sheared the pin on the helm.

The cook came up to see what the war was about, and shortly afterward, smoke came pouring out of the galley.

The steak was burning—not the ship. Having no steerage way we never did find the bird.

As they approached Valparaiso before sunrise, the Andes and Mt. Aconcagua at 23,000 feet were silhouetted against the sky.

This is one of my collector's items, possibly the greatest elevation visible

Peruvian Bird Group
pencil sketch, 17 x 15,
1935.

In 1935, Jaques again visited
the coast of Peru and
sketched the barren, rocky
headlands of South Chincha
Island, capped with thick
deposits of dried guano,
dazzling white in the hot
tropical sun.

from land or sea anywhere. . . . At sunrise it was instantly lost in the haze.

From Chile the *Zaca* headed north to the Peruvian coast and the Chinchas Islands where Lee had been in 1926 studying the great colonies of sea birds on these guano-covered, sun-baked rocks.

It was an interesting experience—sketching with many birds, sea lions visible, [and] the great pelican shadows crossing my drawing board. The shadows of the underparts of the white-bellied birds disappearing as they flew over the white islands.

Hornrigas de Afuera is a small group of sharp rocks collecting a terrific surf. We circled them, and no doubt they had been charted so the Captain knew what he was doing. Nobody, ever, could land there and I, for one, was glad to leave for the Galapagos.

Our first stop in the Galapagos Islands was Post Office Bay. There was a box there where expeditions would leave mail for the next visitors to pick up and mail. Much evidence of picnics ashore, cans and garbage, the usual—you can't win.

There were penguins there too, a variety of the family from the southern and colder parts of the southern hemisphere that was responding to the barely cooler water, the remnant of the Humboldt Current

Marine Iguanas,
Galapagos Islands
scratchboard, 6 x 7½;
illustration for Victor von
Hagen's *South American Zoo*.

which sets west on the Equator. These birds were about as far removed from normal habitat as an astronaut from the earth.

The Whitney Hall exhibit of the Galapagos Islands was collected here, and a peculiar situation developed—Crocker had set a time for our arrival at Panama, and that was more time than I needed. Florence was to meet me in Panama and I wanted—hoped—Crocker would agree to get to Panama sooner, but I would have to let Florence know in time. I knew Crocker wouldn't leave sooner if he knew I wanted to go. It had to be *his* idea. Anyway I didn't put the idea across.

To paint the background sketch, in oil, I went ashore, had a canvas canopy stretched . . . underneath which I worked. When the work was finished I still went ashore each day, promptly, at a given preordered minute by the chronometer. We would all be in the launch waiting for the minute. Once, Toshio, who was very patient, made his only critical remark, "This is ridiculous."

Once I stayed below to annoy Crocker, expecting to come on deck at just the right time but Crocker got excited and sent for me, two minutes early!

And what was I doing—me being the sole reason for going ashore? I was finished with my painting. I took reading matter ashore, sat under my canopy where it was relatively cool, and read all day. A mockingbird sat on top and sang for me.

I knew Crocker's eyesight wasn't good enough to see me from the *Zaca*—even with binoculars.

Well—I think having a yacht with full crew and owner waiting days for me to read something—I wish I knew what it was—is luxury enough for anybody, and with my own private personal mockingbird to supply the music.

When the *Zaca* arrived in Panama City, Lee was greeted by Florence and Dr. Chapman. Most of the museum staff went directly on to New York by steamship, but Lee and Florence spent an extra week with Dr. Chapman on Barro Colorado Island where Lee had collected his first museum group ten years earlier. Florence loved the tropical forest with its flowering trees and bright birds, and they both felt it was like a second honeymoon to paddle along the shores in a native cayuco. "Let's put it this way, a very successful ending to the Crocker Pacific Expedition."

The exhibits for which Lee collected material during the *Zaca* voyage were part of the Whitney Hall of Pacific Birds, then being developed at the American Museum. Lee painted all eighteen habitat groups in this hall, as well as four murals and the large domed ceiling. He was now perfecting the art of diorama painting. He understood the educational objectives of bringing diverse wildlife and natural habitats to an urban audience, but he also recognized the importance that aesthetic quality played in the success of the exhibits. The artist must create the illusion of light, atmosphere, and a vast space within the confines of a small area. The viewer, in turn, must be left with the feeling of being at the scene and, if possible, experience some of the artist's and naturalist's appreciation for the environment and its wildlife.

During the 1920s and 1930s, a number of artists were working

Jaques paints a panorama of the Galapagos Islands on the last stop of the 1935 *Zaca* expedition to the South Pacific; courtesy of the California Academy of Natural Sciences.

on dioramas at the American Museum and at other museums across the country. The technique of diorama painting differed considerably with each artist. One of Lee's contemporary artists took a very mechanical approach to the painting process:

> He laid the sky out in squares of known area, figured the weight or volume of paint required for each area, and the color, mixed it and put it in a flexible tube until he had enough tubes for all the squares, all numbered properly. Then he squeezed the color from each tube and painted it in the proper square and in this way got the gradation in tone and color which he wanted. . . . It took quite a while.
>
> He went into factors of perspective just not necessary in ordinary work. In an art world where perspective is a dirty word.

Lee Jaques had a less rigid approach to diorama painting. He used a simple set of perspective rules, relying on his strong sense

Coatis
pen and ink; illustration for Frank M. Chapman's *Life in an Air Castle*, 1938. Courtesy of American Museum of Natural History.

These relatives of the raccoon were a common sight on Barro Colorado Island. Active by day, and often running in bands, the coatis became expert at robbing Chapman's bird feeders.

of linear and atmospheric perspective to create an effective image. But painting on the curved surface of a diorama background presented special problems:

> From a single selected viewpoint a background sketch could be projected on the sides of a U-shaped space, and in reverse, the finished painting could be photographed to appear correct. But it wouldn't fool the eye. When you are looking at the background, anyone with two good eyes knows just where that wall is, whatever is painted on it.
>
> The horizon of a background painted on a curved surface should be at eye level. At no other level would it appear to be a straight line. Since everyone's eyes are not at the same level, five feet from the floor seems the best compromise.

Often Jaques would make paper cutouts, usually of birds, and attach them to the background to work out problems of composition and perspective before finally painting them in. His purpose was to create an illusion of space and a sense of the birds' movement in that space. Always a pragmatist, he sometimes painted birds or trees over cracks in the background, and when objects

Moose Group
pencil sketch, 7 x 17,
1944.

This sketch was used for a diorama painting at the Bell Museum of Natural History. The notes refer to more detailed sketches of specific areas.

were located at the sharply curved sides of the painting, he distorted their shapes so that they would appear correct. He investigated new lighting techniques, designed better shapes for the background wall, and incorporated mirrors when they added to the desired illusion.

> In painting backgrounds, you have many problems, and if you solve them they are no longer visible, and you get no credit. Only the failures are visible.

At times, Jaques had to paint exhibits of places he had never seen and for which little reference material was available to work from.

> I was given the background painting for the Musk-oxen exhibit to do, the reason being permits to collect musk ox could not be obtained. No one could finance an expensive expedition.
>
> The animals were done from old skins collected on a Peary Expedition. There was no material for the background. Just a surface and paint and me.
>
> In the photographic department I could find no prints that looked like musk ox country. They were from ships, usually, and along shore. Museum policy in the hall was to select a most spectacular background subject. Instead of the plains for the coyote they had Yosemite. I wanted musk ox country in spite of never having seen musk ox country.
>
> I did find finally an old, very faded photo that looked good. But the portfolio from which it came was not labeled—except that the print in which I was interested was labeled "The Bellows," which didn't prove much.
>
> Continuing my search for material in the Museum's library I found, among books on Arctic Exploration in a tiny volume in which, quite by chance, I unfolded a map on which were lettered the words "The

Musk Ox
pencil sketch, 7 x 8½, 1947.

Although Jaques probably never saw a wild musk ox, he had an affinity for this animal of the far north. This is a preparatory sketch for an illustration in Victor Cahalane's *Mammals of North America.*

Bellows." I knew then where "The Bellows" were. The Greely [Expedition] of 1881 had gone to Ellesmere Island. The relief ship, expected the next summer, had failed to arrive. In 1883 the survivors, in small boats, were picked up, and with them, either as film (plates) or as the photo I found, [was] the source material I used for the musk ox background.

The angle of the photo was not great enough for the full, say, 160° I needed so I filled in with a snow squall. A man who had in later years been through that same valley came in the Museum while I was working on the painting and he was enthusiastic about it. It clicked, to the one man of all the millions of the earth's population who had been there and who knew he had been there, it clicked.

That was the kind of reward and sometimes the only reward that made the work worthwhile.

Over the years, Lee had become somewhat disenchanted with the American Museum. He had begun his career there with great enthusiasm and possibly too much idealism. Staff jealousies had developed and with the administrative turnovers of the early forties, the stress became too great. He retired at the earliest possible date, September 1942. He had accomplished some very fine work for the Museum, but felt he had never received the professional freedom and recognition he deserved.

What I have done is the best I could within the limitations and I have enjoyed it. Yet it might have been so much better.

Leaving the Museum was in many ways a great release. Lee continued to paint exhibits on a contract basis for the American

Noel Dunn.

Lee and Florence Jaques are here photographed in the early 1960s in their backyard at North Oaks, Minnesota, where they spent their later years. Their modest house was built between two ponds with a thicket of trees and a small bog nearby. Although they continued to travel and Lee continued to take commissions for exhibits and book illustrations, their activities were increasingly centered here at home. Through the 1950s and 1960s, Lee devoted much of his time to his miniature railroad and to his paintings.

Museum and for several other institutions across the country. He did exhibits for the Boston Museum of Science, the Peabody Museum at Yale, the University of Nebraska Museum, and the Welder Wildlife Foundation in Texas. With increasing frequency, Lee returned to Minnesota to paint exhibits for the James Ford Bell Museum of Natural History at the University of Minnesota (then the Minnesota Museum of Natural History), and Lee and Florence were to return to Minnesota permanently in 1953.

During the later years in New York, Lee and Florence had more time to indulge their love for travel and develop their partnership as author and artist. Canoe Country was published in 1938. It was followed by The Geese Fly High (1939) and Birds Across the Sky (1942). Both books describe their travels and birdwatching adventures during Lee's years with the American Museum. Soon after leaving the Museum, Lee and Florence were given a fellowship by the University of Minnesota Press to spend a winter on Minnesota's Canadian border and write a companion book to Canoe Country. The result was Snowshoe Country, and in 1946 they won the John Burroughs medal for their outstanding work in nature literature. Their last books together were Canadian Spring (1947) and As Far as the Yukon (1951).

The 1940s and 1950s were a peak time for Lee's career as an illustrator of nature and wildlife books. He did drawings for South American Zoo by Victor von Hagen, Mammals of North America by Victor Cahalane, S. Dillon Ripley's A Paddling of Ducks, and William O. Douglas's My Wilderness: The Pacific West, and many others. While on the fellowship for Snowshoe Country, Lee and Florence met Sigurd Olson, who was writing about his own experience in the Quetico-Superior region. Three of Olson's books, The Singing Wilderness, Listening Point, and The Lonely Land, are graced with Jaques drawings and demonstrate the two men's mutual love for this unique wilderness of forests and lakes.

Almost all of these book illustrations were drawn in the scratchboard medium, which Lee learned from his earlier experience as a commercial artist in Duluth. The technique uses a chalk or clay-coated board on which the artist draws with black ink. Once the ink has dried, it can be scratched with a sharp tool to create white lines in an otherwise dark area. The technique can quickly create a strong image with an appearance that is something of a hybrid between wood-engraving and pen and ink drawing.

The wood-engraving process dominated black and white illustrations for much of the nineteenth century, but with the development of photo-mechanical printing processes, a black and white line drawing could be reproduced directly without the need for an engraver. This gave new freedom to the artist, and the late nineteenth and early twentieth century was the heyday for pen-and-ink drawing. Many artists were placing new emphasis on the design of dark and light spaces, and on the quality and pattern of the lines themselves. However, most commercial work was still dominated by the traditions of wood engraving, where the artist

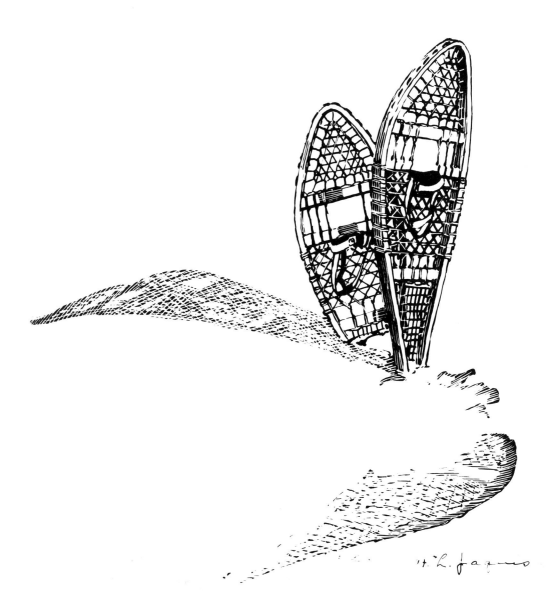

Snowshoes
scratchboard, 7½ x 7½;
illustration from *Snowshoe
Country* by F. P. Jaques.

used fine lines to duplicate the effect of gray areas, and strove to include as much detail as possible.

As a commercial artist in the early 1920s, Lee was apprenticed into this traditional standard where quality was judged by the fineness of lines and the quantity of detail. "Most of my work was for Marshall Wells: labels, drawings of bicycles, lamps, anything. . . . Penwork in such meticulous detail I couldn't approach it now."

Although Jaques did some very fine pen work, in scratchboard drawing he found a medium better suited to the expression of those things he found so appealing in nature: strong shapes, stark contrasts, and open spaces. His drawings are masterpieces of selectivity, carefully composed of dark areas and white spaces, interwoven with patches of boldly scratched lines. Through the reduction to black and white, Jaques dramatized the effects of light and shadow. His black lines and shapes capture the distilled essence of the natural objects they represent. Whether his subjects were grass, water, trees, or birds, he was able to define them with a few lines or a silhouette. The large white spaces give the

Cheakamus Canyon near Fraser Pass
scratchboard, 12 x 8½.

One spring, Lee and Florence crossed the North American Continent traveling mostly by train, and eventually descended the upper Yukon River by sternwheeler. Florence wrote of their adventures exploring the "wild gardens" along the way in *As Far as the Yukon.*

drawings a sense of openness and depth that invites the eye to explore. The patterned lines bridge the black and white areas creating an overall image of remarkable structure and vibrancy. The finished drawing is representational and yet a work of strong

Canvasbacks
scratchboard; illustration for
Florence Page Jaques's *The
Geese Fly High*, 1939.
Courtesy of Alexander Hoffman.

abstract design. Jaques's illustrations started a small revival of scratchboard drawing and introduced the technique to wildlife art. "Based on my experience with chalkboard in commercial art days, I did the drawings in *Mammals of North America* in scratchboard and that started a considerable number of wildlife artists using it."

His scratchboard drawings were strikingly different, not only because of their strong design, but also because of the way they handled form, a traditional problem in animal illustration. Conventionally, form is described in two-dimensional art by the use of shading, using various gray tones to reproduce the play of light and shadow on the subject. However, many animals are darkly colored above and white or lightly colored underneath. When lit naturally from the sun and sky, the dark upper surfaces are brightly illuminated and the light lower parts thrown in shadow. This natural countershading of many animals tends to produce a uniform shade over their entire body. Their volume is thus disguised, making them more difficult to be seen by predators or prey. Although many other factors influence animal coloration, often when an artist faithfully renders the light and shadow on an animal, its natural countershading hampers the depiction of its form.

A further complication is that in drawings used for illustrations in ornithology books, the shadows on the white undersides of birds could be confused for coloration. During the early part of the century, many natural history artists worked directly for professional scientists, who often had their own biases.

> The countershading was a thorn in the bird artist's side. The ornithologists of the day were determined not to accept anything in a painting for white but white paper.
>
> Which meant that a painted bird could be nothing but a map. These white-for-white dumbs joined with the people who refused to accept snow shadows. And these people were closely allied with those who refused to accept correct perspective.

For these and other reasons, most natural history artists still tend to concentrate on the superficial details of their subjects, such as the texture and coloration of fur or the number and position of feathers. Form, if described at all, is indicated by changes in the outlines of feathers or by reduced and conventionalized shading.

In his scratchboard drawings, Jaques took a very different approach to this problem of animal form. He would first make use of the shape and position of strong shadows to reveal volume. But often, surfaces of his animals seem to be divided into a series of planes. The direction of the scratched lines gives the planes curvature and orientation in space. The relation of one plane to the next builds a sense of volume into the subject that could not be achieved by shading or feather detail alone. He emphasizes the changes in contour of the surface, in essentially the same analytical way he treats landscapes.

Thus his animals, particularly his mammals, often look chunky or chiseled, as if they were roughly sculpted. This can be seen in his paintings as well, such as in *The Wolf Pack* and *The Jack Rabbit*. The effect is, of course, a distortion of surface appearance, but it reveals much about the animal's underlying structure, and to be effective this process requires the artist to have a good knowledge of the living anatomy of each animal. In *Mammals of North America*, Jaques had to draw many species whose anatomy and posture were unfamiliar to him, and some of his drawings clearly fail for this reason. Nevertheless, the drawings and paintings of Jaques often reveal an understanding of animal form as keen as that of Carl Rungius who specialized in painting just a few species of large game mammals. Despite his ability to vividly depict the forms of animals and their habitats, this was never Jaques's singular concern. One hallmark of his work, most clearly seen in his scratchboard drawings, is a concern for the purely aesthetic and decorative quality of his finished image.

Jaques illustrated a number of books with watercolors and oil paintings as well as with scratchboards. Color plates by Jaques

Barren Ground Caribou
scratchboard, 11½ x 8;
illustration from *Mammals
of North America*, by Victor
H. Cahalane; courtesy of
Paul Snyder.

can be found in books such as *The Birds of Minnesota*, by Thomas
S. Roberts (1934); *Oceanic Birds of South America* by Robert
Cushman Murphy (1935); and *Outdoor Life's Gallery of North
American Game* (1946). These paintings are much closer to traditional bird art and wildlife painting than are Jaques scratchboards, and yet a distinctive Jaques style is always evident. To
understand the significance of Jaques's work, it must be seen in
relation to the traditions of bird and wildlife art in which he
worked.

Although wildlife art today has become an immensely popular

and often profitable enterprise, it still remains largely separated from what is academically considered fine art. Despite modern views that consider subject matter insignificant in determining the quality of a work of art (thus allowing soup cans, for instance, to be art), renditions of wild animals continue to suffer from a prejudice that has excluded them from consideration as true art in Western culture. However, domestic animals, such as horses and dogs and dead game in the form of still lifes, were acceptable and were favorite subjects of many Dutch and Flemish artists. In the rare instances where wild animals were portrayed, they were usually in totally unnatural situations and used for allegorical purposes. In the works of Rubens and Delacroix, lions and tigers were symbols of rage unleashed as they struggled in gory conflict with horse and rider. When used as symbols of human emotions and values, animals were acceptable as art, but rarely was an interest expressed in the true description of the animal itself—its structure, its behavior, its natural history. The few early artists and naturalists who did draw wildlife were quite often guilty of the reverse situation. They dealt primarily with the identity and classification of particular species, and their main concern was for scientific draftsmanship, as in the case of ornithologists' requiring artists to produce "birdmaps."

Despite the often conflicting demands of art and science, a small number of artists of both ancient and modern civilizations have successfully combined aesthetics with the desire to portray nature accurately. The earliest known art, the paleolithic cave paintings of Europe, remain among the most vital and authentic depictions of wildlife ever produced. Expressive yet essentially accurate images of bison, horses, and reindeer are drawn across the cave walls with but scant traces of man. Of the early civilizations, the Egyptians were remarkable for their awareness of wild animals, as is evident in the representations of their gods, who were given animal characteristics and identities. Egyptian artists also executed numerous works with ordinary animals as their subjects, and were the first to portray plant life as an integral part of each animal scene. The Minoans of the ancient Aegean used many animal motifs, particularly sea creatures such as dolphins and octopi, on their pottery and frescoes; their designs evoke a sense of the movement and freedom of wild animals. The Romans and the Chinese, too, placed much emphasis on naturalism and the close observation of animals.

Some examples of Medieval and Renaissance works of art, mainly birds, also reveal accurate observation of natural objects by the artist. These efforts were furthered during the intellectual awakening of the Renaissance, with its intense curiosity concerning all things. Many of the works of Antonio Pisanello and Albrecht Dürer are combinations of naturalism, art, and science. Nevertheless, the classical traditions eventually restricted the subjects of art to the concerns of humans. More objective interests in nature, beyond human cultural experience, were relegated to science.

Passenger Pigeons and Mourning Doves
watercolor, 12 x 9, early 1930s.

In this illustration for Thomas S. Roberts's *The Birds of Minnesota*, Jaques produced accurate ornithological rendering in a composition that can be enjoyed as a purely aesthetic experience.

Later advances in science generated a need for presenting facts in pictorial form, and during the sixteenth and seventeenth centuries, the depictions of mythical and fantastic beasts were gradually replaced by more rational images from zoological science. In the seventeenth century, naturalists became increasingly interested in discovering and describing new species from throughout the world. Artists were put to the task of accurately portraying as many of the taxonomic characteristics of each species as possible. They were now working from real objects rather than their imaginations. Unfortunately, these objects were usually dead, often poorly preserved specimens and most scientific illustrations of the period lack any sense for the living animals. Birds and mammals often were placed in unnatural postures and inappropriate surroundings.

Toward the end of the eighteenth century, a few illustrators once again began to combine the curiosity and knowledge of a naturalist with the sensitivity of an artist. Thomas Bewick, who is best known for his technical accomplishments in the art of wood engraving, represents this trend. In his small engravings of British birds and mammals, Bewick demonstrates an understanding and sympathy for living animals. He spent many hours watching animals in the field and established feeding stations to observe birds more closely. His images are modest, warm, and sincere and display a sensibility for the animals' natural surroundings.

This union of artist and naturalist is best seen in the work of those illustrators inspired by the exploration and colonization of the New World. Here western culture was confronted with a diversity of wildlife and wilderness that had long been lost in domesticated Europe. The naturalist Mark Catesby did his own engravings for his *Natural History of Carolina, Florida and the Bahama Islands 1731-43*. His plates, although crude by present standards, demonstrate the enthusiasm of a naturalist exploring the life of new and wild lands. This growing desire to document the beauty and diversity of America's native animals inspired Alexander Wilson (1766-1813), who produced the first major illustrated work on American birds.

Probably the most universally recognized artist-naturalist was John James Audubon (1785-1857). Born in Haiti and educated in France where he received some artistic training, he came to America at eighteen to oversee his father's property outside Philadelphia. However, Audubon spent most of his time hunting, collecting, and drawing the animals, particularly birds, of the area. He slowly developed his ability to handle watercolors and chalks, and he devised a method of posing freshly killed birds with wires to record the detail of their plumage in lifelike positions. Only after years of failed business ventures did he devote his life to his passion for painting birds and his dream of publishing the great folio "Birds of America." The effort was monumental, including over a thousand birds drawn life size and in color, with a life history given for each. Audubon's genius, though, was the artistic quality of his images which far surpassed that of his predecessors. His drawings vibrate with life and energy, as the birds turn, twist, dive, and hunt. Through skilled linear drawing and occasional use of light and shade, Audubon endows his birds with substance. Each plate is beautifully composed, with foliage and backgrounds added not only to indicate the natural surroundings of the birds, but also to build dynamic design and color harmony. If Audubon's birds are occasionally in awkward or overly dramatic positions, one must remember he worked in a period of romantic art trends, where the imagination and memory had to fill the role later played by photography, in recording instantaneous moments. Audubon's achievement was to establish animal portraiture as an art and lay the foundation for all artist-naturalists to follow.

Charged with the same enthusiasm possessed by Audubon, Louis Agassiz Fuertes (1874-1927) had a remarkably thorough understanding of the birds he painted. He carried Audubon's tradition of bird portraiture to its highest development. Fuertes painted more objectively than did Audubon. His birds are perfectly structured and are unrivaled as textbook illustrations for both the amateur and professional naturalist. Fuertes's portrayals are uncomplicated and appear as though one were observing the animal from only a short distance away. His genius was in his ability to capture the essence of the living animal in his paintings. Not only are the feathers drawn correctly, but the subtle postures and gestures are those that experienced field observers recognize as characteristics of particular species. Despite his perfectly observed birds, however, Fuertes's compositions lack the strong sense of design inherent in Audubon's. He spent most of his career illustrating textbooks and bird guides, for which he was always in demand. His paintings were beautiful animal portraits, usually against a plain background, but his attempts to include more of a landscape were generally unsuccessful. Fuertes was aware of this problem and wanted to abandon illustration altogether to concentrate on painting landscapes with animals in them. Unfortunately, his premature death prevented his doing so.

In many respects, Francis Lee Jaques accomplished what Fuertes hoped to do. He, too, was extremely concerned with the essence of his animal subjects. He worked from a thorough knowledge of wildlife gained from years as a hunter, taxidermist, lumberjack, bird watcher, and draftsman. His work had, as Sigurd Olson put it, "authenticity and absolute integrity that could not abide carelessness in any form."

Unlike Audubon and Fuertes, Jaques did not seek to depict animals through the meticulous description of surface detail. He refused to become a "feather painter" and used details of feathers and textures only where absolutely necessary. He felt that details that are largely meaningless were often used by artists to disguise a poor understanding of the living animal. Instead, he sought to define the essence of a bird, or any other part of nature, by extracting and amplifying its characteristic shape and form.

> The shape of things has always given me the most intense satisfaction. Such beauty one wants to preserve—to make it available, as far as one can, to others. There are many paths, some devious, to the same ultimate goal. I speak of my particular path; it was the short cut—just paint the thing as it looks, only if possible, *more so*."

Jaques also was fascinated by the structure and pattern of

Great Blue Herons over Dyke Marsh
scratchboard; illustration from *Spring in Washington*, by Louis Joseph Halle, Jr., 1947. Courtesy Audubon Naturalist Society.

animals in motion, especially birds in flight. As a child he loved to watch waterfowl flying from the nearby creeks or passing overhead in the great fall migrations. The large dome with flying birds that he painted when he first came to the American Museum expressed some of this joy and was an artistic breakthrough for its time.

> Brooks, Fuertes, and Horsfall were doing most of the bird portraits of the day. This was before color, or high speed photography. None of them did good birds in flight. . . . I suspect that at the time I understood bird flight better than any of them.

Some of the most accurate paintings of birds in flight were then being done for sporting magazines. Two early artists that Jaques admired were Belmore Brown, who also did many fine museum backgrounds, and his son, George.

> Belmore Brown I used to see at the Salamagundi Club, and I liked him and his paintings – western mountains, etc.
> I fear I was a little jealous of George Brown's work, [as] I don't believe I was of any other artist. His work was a breakthrough. It was different and better. He did living birds in a landscape.

Jaques, however, did not paint flying birds from the perspective of a hunter sighting down a gun barrel. His birds are seen through the eyes of a naturalist, as much concerned with the environment through which they move as with the animals themselves. In his painting *Egrets in Cypress Swamp* one can sense the slow beat of the birds' wings as they alternate from shadow to the glistening light of the evening sun. The path of the birds through the ancient and broken trees can be traced, but it is

Egrets in Cypress Swamp
oil on canvas, 30 x 24,
1953. Courtesy Dr. Burt
Brent.

the trees, the still air and water, and the falling of twilight that
dominate the image.

One artist who very successfully combined wildlife and landscape was the Swedish painter Bruno Liljefors. Trained at the
Royal Academy in Stockholm, where less bias was felt against
wild animals in art, he pursued his love of wildlife in his paintings. Best known for his eagles and sea ducks, but by no means
limited to them, Liljefors painted his animals within intimate
landscapes. Waves, rocks, grass, or snow are close at hand and

often nearly envelop the animal subjects. He painted in a broad, open style with great emphasis on light and, in his later paintings, color. The shapes and edges of his animals and landscapes are diffuse and yet masterfully observed. He used this style to convey a powerful sense of movement in his animals. In his famous painting *White Hare*, the rabbit seems to be caught at an instant between either dissolving into the snowy landscape or leaping out of the canvas.

In comparison, Jaques's work is much more delineated, with harder, more well-defined edges. His rocks, trees, grasses, and other elements of the landscape are focused and identifiable and yet a holistic image is still achieved. Although his landscapes usually are broad and expansive, they are never merely backdrops for a spotlighted animal. These differences in interest and style were complemented and nurtured by Jaques's experiences as a museum artist. Diorama exhibits required an emphasis on the environment and the accurate depiction of all its parts. The museum also exposed him to the movements for conservation and wilderness preservation, which had a strong influence on his work.

A general appreciation for wilderness has not always existed in American culture. The early colonists and later pioneers carried with them traditional European attitudes toward wild, unsettled lands. The American wilderness was seen as a wasteland, an enemy to be conquered and put to useful purpose for the material benefit of humans. Nevertheless, wilderness in America had some early admirers. The eighteenth-century naturalists Mark Catesby and John and William Bartram expressed a much more sympathetic view of wilderness, seeing it as the reflection of God's work, unspoiled by humans. With the growth of the Romantic movement in the early nineteenth century, the wilderness qualities of solitude, vastness, and mystery once despised by Puritan colonists became desirable to the Romantic mind. Writers such as Emerson and Thoreau began to redefine wild nature as a tonic for the human intellect and spirit, and a release from the artificial constraints of civilization.

The vast wilderness resources of America also were seen as the one major and unique advantage over Europe. This insight helped fill America's psychological need to find an identity distinct from that of the Old World. The demonstration of the quality and beauty of America's natural resources provided inspiration for Wilson and Audubon. Audubon's extraordinary success was in part due to the incorporation of Romantic sentiment into the dramatic action and expressions of his birds. Audubon played the part, to great advantage in Europe, of an American frontiersman whose genius was inspired by his contact with the purifying wilderness. His achievement of establishing a popular appreciation for the beauty of wildlife has long outlived the Romantic Period.

Audubon was one of a growing number of painters who looked to the American wilderness as a source of artistic inspiration. In

Caribou on Ice
oil on canvas, 30 x 36,
late 1940s.

As a mist of ice crystals falls,
woodland caribou walk
along the frozen shore of
Gunflint Lake, at a time
before the forests of the
canoe country were cut and
burned.

particular, the work of Thomas Cole and the Hudson River School artists was a visual expression of the Romantic view of wilderness and its association with the American identity. By the middle of the 1800s, this school of thought praised contact with wilderness as being responsible for the positive attributes of the American character.

However, the reality of the nineteenth century was the widespread destruction of wilderness all across the North American continent. Most people believed, as many still do, that destruction of wildlife and wild places meant progress, and that unbridled exploitation of natural resources was the proper work of humans on earth. With unprecedented speed, the forests were cut, the prairies plowed, and the great herds and flocks of wildlife slaughtered. For much of the century, people solved the problems of depleted resources simply by moving farther west. Wild, open lands were rapidly being replaced by farms, mines, mills, and cities. Eventually, to a growing number of people, apprecia-

tion for nature was not enough. Action was essential to conserve
the natural resources that provided America's prosperity, and to
preserve the shrinking wilderness areas for the recreational
benefits they afforded.

A major proponent of this early conservation movement was
John Muir. He became the publicizer of the philosophy of Emerson and Thoreau. Better versed than these authors in the
sciences, Muir combined his writings on the values of wilderness
with descriptions of botany and geology. He extolled the beauty
and undisturbed harmony of wild nature, and promoted the view
that wild animals had worth and a right to an independent existence without being measured by their material value to humans.
Through his writings he spearheaded a movement to preserve
undeveloped areas of the country as wilderness parks. By the turn
of the century, Muir and the advocates for the wise use of forest
lands and resources had established a strong conservation sentiment in America.

During the same period, Lee Jaques was growing up on the
plains of Kansas and the north woods of Minnesota. He had an
intimate knowledge of what it meant to carve out a living on the
fringe of the wilderness. As a boy, plowing the prairies of Kansas,
Lee's concerns, like those of most people, were for the immediate
problems of surviving.

> A small patch of corn was on a slope, and I remember worrying during a
> heavy rain, about the immediate hills of corn washing out — it didn't occur to me [that] the top soil — a thin rich layer of black soil built up over
> many thousands of years by the prairie grasses, was going too. Neither
> did [it occur to] a thoughtless nation.

In Minnesota he cut trees and cleared the land, but only later
did he become aware of the full consequences of such actions.

The Mine at Flin Flon
scratchboard, 6½ x 8½

Illustration for Florence
Page Jaques's *Canadian
Spring*, 1947.

The pine belt extended from Maine across northern New York, Ontario, Michigan, Wisconsin, and Minnesota. In the East the deciduous forest reseeded itself, but in Michigan, Wisconsin, and Minnesota (Ontario, too?) when the timber was cut, fires, which no one attempted to control, burned the soil. There are almost no pines now in this belt, which starts (its south edge) just a few miles north of here—mills were at Stillwater, Minneapolis, and downriver to St. Louis, up river, St. Cloud and Brainerd.

I know. I know—the country had to be developed but we developed it very wastefully—we might have made it beautiful. It is, so far as we could make it, ugly. I won't try to list the ugly things—they are visible.

Jaques's migration from a small pioneer farm to Duluth and finally to New York City paralleled a general trend of urbanization during the twentieth century. As wilderness became scarce, its value grew as a place to find spiritual revival from the pressures of civilization. Lee felt the restrictions of city life and was deeply concerned about the loss of access to wild and open areas.

Much of the Land of the Free is closed to the public. About a third of the state of Maine belongs to the Great Northern Paper Company . . . probably that is good. It is wilderness. The wide-open spaces can be seen over the fences. Many of the older roads of the west are fenced off by the cattlemen. Locked in a freeway at 70 m.p.h. is not a good way to see America. The contours visible are those of the bulldozers, and the old roads are fenced off.

Many of the books Jaques illustrated dealt with the theme of wilderness as a beneficial influence on the human character. Sigurd Olson returned to the ideas of Thoreau and concluded that the best life should allow contact with both civilization and wilderness, in that neither one can be truly appreciated without the other. William O. Douglas in his books on the environment explored the values of wilderness in maintaining a free society. He saw the effects of wilderness experience in building self-reliance, confidence, and individualism as important in helping to free people from the mass pressures of modern society that could lead to totalitarian tendencies.

Lee had a great need for open, uninhabited space to recharge his spirit, to provide personal peace and freedom. Florence felt that Lee's work expressed this renewal and uplifting of the human spirit in contact with wilderness. The large open areas in his works evoke a sense of depth and freedom. His success in portraying a feeling of motion in his animals is in large part accomplished by giving them room to move in. His flying birds are never trapped within tight compositions filled with extraneous detail. They have air around them and space from which they have come and space into which they are about to move. In some paintings the sense of anticipated motion is so strong, as with the magpie in *The Road West*, that the effect can be disconcerting.

The need to find wildlife and open areas, to revive the spirit and reassert personal freedom is as strong today as ever. Yearly, millions of Americans seek a wilderness experience of some sort. This present popularity of wilderness and support for its preservation has been bolstered by ecological principles that naturalists

The Road West
oil on canvas, 30 x 36,
1966.

Lee and Florence Jaques
reveled in the open spaces of
the Canadian great plains.
Once, while slowly driving
on a gravel road looking for
birds or other wildlife, they
came over a slight rise and
there, suddenly, were the
Rockies.

were defining during the period in which Jaques was a museum artist. The knowledge that animals are found in characteristic places or habitats is as ancient as hunting. However, the significance of this fact was not really understood until scientists began looking more closely at the characteristic groupings of plants and animals known as communities. Gradually, naturalists shifted their interest from simply documenting natural diversity to exploring scientific explanations for it. Evolutionary theory affirmed that all of life was in fact related, and that species were shaped by the interactions among organisms and between organisms and their physical environments. The study of these interrelationships is ecology, and its development led to a new view of life that recognized environments as living systems. Aldo Leopold, one of the first promoters of ecology, stressed the interdependence of all parts of a living environment. Often changes in one aspect of an environment produce changes elsewhere that cannot be predicted without an understanding of nature as a system. This ecological perspective deeply affected Jaques's attitudes and conceptions of the environments he painted.

The prairies were maintained by fire—which prevented the encroachment of the forests. The grasslands built up a tough sod (so tough houses were built of it), which prevented erosion and permitted the growth of a short, whitish grass, the buffalo grass, which was very nourishing. Millions of buffalo lived on the grasslands, fertilized them, and died

66

there. Nothing was removed—nothing wasted. The perfectly balanced mid-continent.

Then the settlement and the plow, and the soil was exposed to the rains, and much of the rich soil built up over many thousands of years is gone. I admit I didn't foresee this, worrying only about the one immediate crop. We mined the land, plowed grasslands that never should have been broken, killed the rich native grasses—which if replaced at all is with inferior grasses.

True with irrigation and fertilizers we raise larger crops than ever before—but one suspects fertilizers are [exhaustable], and we've washed our own down the rivers and into each others drinking water. And much of the soil is gone. We've extended the deserts by hundreds of thousands of square miles.

In the light of ecology, wilderness areas are needed not only for the healthful recreation they provide but also for the basic scientific information they hold about the world around us. As undisturbed environments, they serve as references for measuring the effects of human activity. Wilderness areas are irreplaceable reservoirs of information for future generations, and may well hold answers to questions we have not yet learned to ask. In creating his diorama exhibits, Jaques hoped to preserve for the public a view of environments before they were disturbed or destroyed.

We've needed a great North American Museum, showing what North America *was*, and as a yardstick to show what we have done to it in a very brief time.

The Jackrabbit
oil on canvas, 24 x 30, c. 1950.

Jaques painted this solitary jackrabbit silhouetted against the sky as it stands on the edge between wild prairie and plowed field.

Egret in Florida Pond
oil on canvas, 24 x 28,
c. 1935.

Jaques's methods in painting nature parallel those of an ecologist in studying it. The first step in analyzing an environment is to define what is there. Representative samples of plants and animals need to be identified and counted and conditions of climate, soil, and other physical factors monitored. Specific ecological interactions such as between predator and prey or soil and vegetation are studied. The ecologist then seeks relationships between these interactions and the observed patterns of distribution and abundance of life, and from these separate pieces, builds a better understanding of the environment as a system.

In creating a painting, particularly one for an exhibit, Jaques carefully observed and defined representative components of the scene, recording characteristics of water, soil, and landforms. Conditions of weather and time of day are expressed with his distinctive use of color and light. The interactions between these pieces are understood and they are combined with a sensitivity to their aesthetic and ecological relationships. In the painting *Egret*

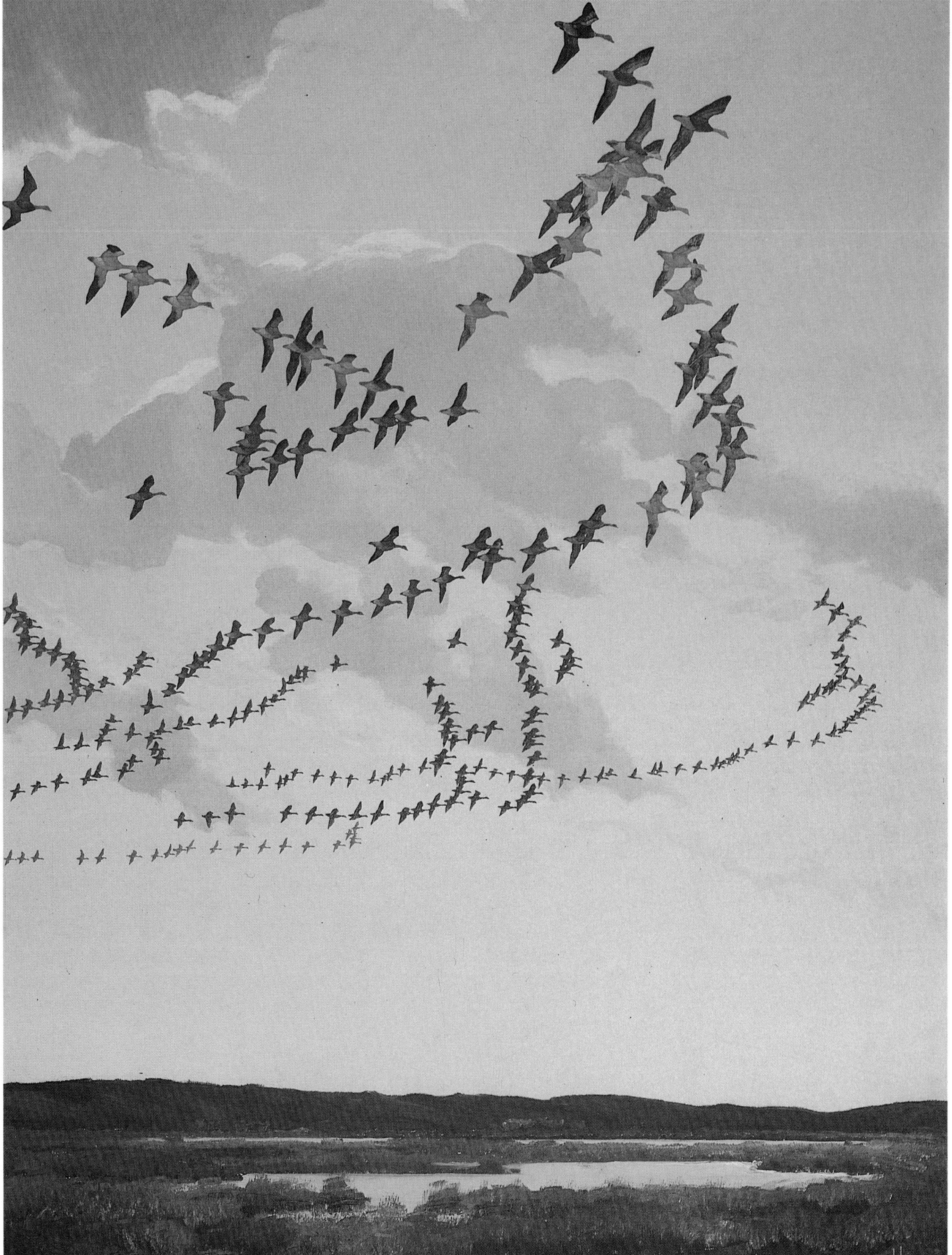
F.L.JAQUES

in Florida Pond, the bird is stalking its aquatic prey at the water's edge. This alone would be a fairly obvious statement about the egret and its habitat. However, the image is enriched with other meaning. The red of the mud is typical of the highly oxidized soils of the south, and on slightly higher ground are stands of southern pines, almost certainly slash pines. Their lower trunks are free of branches, allowing a thick growth of understory shrubs. A sense of heat and humidity permeates the entire image. The finished painting is an integrated system of distinct parts that expresses a deep felt glory in natural beauty as well as a vision of nature as an ecological system.

In early critiques of Jaques's work, he is considered only within the framework of bird or wildlife art, despite his insistence that he was a painter of environments. This aspect of his work was not widely recognized until the environmental movement popularized the concepts of ecology. In the early 1970s, Robert Larson, another museum artist who admired the work of Jaques, identified his aims when he wrote: "Jaques saw the whole ecological panorama—there was rhythm and balance in his work, just as nature intended" (Larson, Robert, "F. L. Jaques, His Artistry and Influence," *Naturalist*, vol. 21, no. 1, 1970 p. 2). Tony Angell, a young wildlife artist at the time, had a similar interpretation of Jaques. "Perhaps he is the first such artist to recognize closely the interrelationships of all life. I find his work expressive of a profound ecological conscience" (Jaques, Florence Page, *Francis Lee Jaques: Artist of the Wilderness World*, 1973, p. 245).

When Jaques was writing his autobiography in 1966 and 1967, the popular conception of ecology was changing; no longer seen as dealing only with wild animals and wilderness, ecology was emerging as a science that held potential answers to problems that threatened the survival of humankind. The magnitude of the environmental crisis forced a recognition that even humanity was a dependent part of natural systems.

> Many dedicated people are interested in conservation but the despoilers are far ahead, and gaining, and conservation will have to lose, as the population grows. And evolution, which created us all, will be stopped in its tracks. There isn't time.
>
> I see a world with rapidly increasing numbers of people who will not, of themselves, do anything to reduce the population explosion.
>
> Is there any evidence the use of insecticides will decrease? Has air pollution decreased anywhere? Has water pollution? We've done wonders in the medical field—but is the *race* any more likely to survive?
>
> I see a world in which it is evident that if we ever have anything approaching peace (and we'd better have) we will have to get along with each other.

The pessimism that often marks Jaques's words reflects not only an awareness of modern environmental problems but also of other disturbing changes in American society. Although he had long used cars to escape the city for trips to natural spots in the surrounding area, he realized that the expanded use of the automobile and the suburban development that it created were rapidly destroying both the city and the open countryside.

Wings Across the Sky
oil on canvas, 40 x 30,
c. 1935.

Great wavy lines of Snow and Blue Geese wing over a prairie marsh on their migration between the Gulf coast and the Arctic tundra. The preservation of habitat for these and many other migratory species is an ongoing conservation problem.

The Old West Passes
oil on canvas, 24 x 30, 1968.

This abandoned barn and hayrake reminded Jaques of the small Kansas farms and great flocks of waterfowl he knew in his youth. In this, his last painting, he felt he had finally achieved the best arrangement of geese in flight.

I sit in the parking lot at the Red Owl supermarket and wait for Florence to buy a package of potato chips or something and think of a European type village built on the area of the parking lot where all the facilities might be found within easy walking distance and where there would be more privacy than in the usual suburban sprawl.

Jaques was a political maverick who was always hoping to reform the world. While working on the railroads in Minnesota, he was once on the ballot as a presidential elector for Eugene V. Debs. In the 1960s, nearing the end of his life, he was deeply troubled by the escalation of what he considered a "wholly unjustified" war in Vietnam. To him, these were simply more signs of the loss of a way of life he once knew. Possibly as a response, he began to paint more images from his own past. Paintings such as *The Cloud* are autobiographical, and others document the decline of family farming and railroading, which were so important in his youth. These are sentimental and nostalgic images, but they are also authentic. Never did he try to reconstruct a past he did not know through experience.

A look at paintings such as *Cold Morning* and *The Old West Passes* point to a major difference between Jaques and most other wildlife painters. He was not interested simply in creating idealized images of wild animals and landscapes. His later paintings express a deep sense of regret for the loss of the closer relationship people once had to the land.

The exploration of the relationship between humanity and

nature has been a strong theme in American art ever since the Hudson River School. In their effort to glorify America's natural wonders, these artists painted romanticized images of spectacular mountains and valleys glowing with a gilded light. By the middle of the nineteenth century, this Romantic movement had largely run its course. The second half of the century was marked by a group of painters who, with little formal artistic training, created a more naturalistic vision of America. They began to paint outdoors and concentrated on natural light and ordinary scenes of people and nature. Most of these Realist painters also worked as illustrators, receiving a practical experience in careful observation.

This shift from Romantic sentiment to the realistic description of sensation is best seen in the work of Winslow Homer. He began his career as an illustrator, and during the Civil War worked for *Harper's Weekly* where he learned to record the essential elements of a scene rapidly and with accuracy. His early paintings of drab camp scenes and plain country settings were widely criticized for what were then considered homely subjects and unfinished technique. His naturalism and love for the outdoors stimulated him to draw many of his visions directly from nature. To him, painting was the realistic representation of nature, but with all fussy details eliminated. Through his vivid art, Homer conveyed the sensations of nature in all its forms, be it a raging northern sea, or a quiet Adirondack pond.

Fredrick Remington and N. C. Wyeth, also were part of this realistic movement. Both spent much of their careers as illustrators. Remington was determined to achieve perfect authenticity in his scenes of western frontier life; to capture the rapid action, he developed the ability to store details in his mind and quickly record all essential facts in sketches. N. C. Wyeth also stressed the importance of gaining direct experience, in order to build an abundant repository of impressions from which to paint. Like the Hudson River painters, he admired Thoreau and viewed nature as a cosmos, inexhaustible in its potential for beauty.

Homer, Remington, Wyeth, and many other artists of the period explored humans' relationship to nature by painting events in the lives of people who lived closest to it. To express their feelings, these artists relied on their innate sense of decorative values. To them, lines, shapes, and colors were not only a means of representing reality, but were a source of aesthetic and sensuous pleasure. By the turn of the century, the methods and style of these realist painters dominated American art and illustration, and Jaques from an early age was strongly influenced by their work:

> This period was in what I call the golden age of illustration. The better magazines were illustrated by a group of great men. And their work is to me, still tops.

Their methods, based so strongly on direct and accurate observation, were very close to the way artist-naturalists worked. Jaques followed their example in manipulating strong colors and

Helper at Hudson
oil on canvas, 20 x 24, 1960; courtesy of Mrs. Patricia Young.

The strong lines, bright sunlight, and deep shadows of this painting create a stark and powerful design, which seems to frame and isolate this old helper locomotive at Hudson, Wisconsin.

well-defined shapes when building powerful designs into his work. His decorative style, deft placement, and ability to simplify objects to their essential forms are all indicative of a similar development and sensibility. Of course, images of wildlife and wilderness predominate, but many clear references are made to human influence. Jaques's particular interest was the interactions of humans and nature in his native Kansas and Minnesota. Prairie farms, grain elevators, lumber camps, and especially railroads are often subjects of his paintings and drawings. In this way, he is identifiable with the artists of the "American Scene," who during the early twentieth century attempted to establish an artistic style independent of the European academic tradition. They dealt with such phenomena as the development of American urban centers and the people who lived in them, in addition to what remained of the frontier. As Jaques once stated:

> The painting of industrial scenes would have interested me very much—steel mills, mines, possibly workmen, logging scenes and railroad subjects. I think I could have spent a lifetime at that, painting smoke, and steam and air pollution.

This type of subject matter brings to mind the Precisionist artists such as Charles Demuth, Charles Sheeler, Joseph Stella, and Georgia O'Keeffe. They documented the growth of the city in their renditions of elevators, smokestacks, bridges, skyscrapers, and other structures associated with urbanization and in-

Golden Twilight:
Baldpates
oil on canvas, 42 x 30,
c. 1935.

dustrialization. Jaques, however, painted the impact of these forces on the wild and rural areas he knew so well. His work is sometimes reminiscent of Edward Hopper and Andrew Wyeth, in that he often projects a strong sense of isolation and remoteness as well as a nostalgic look at a simpler past.

Jaques was aware of and undoubtedly influenced by many of these artistic trends, and was sensitive to the objectives of modernist painters. "When I wake up in the morning, and my wife's closet (or mine) is open, I get the impression of a perfectly gorgeous modern [painting]." However, he still viewed himself primarily as an illustrator who used realism to express his deep felt emotions, as well as accurate information about nature. These varied influences make the art of Jaques difficult to analyze. It is not easily placed within any established category. Much of his work may have suffered from being lost within the gulf that still separates wildlife art from the rest of the artistic world, and a greater awareness of his art may help fill this gap.

In Jaques's paintings, we see natural environments both as a vital component of the American scene and as an endangered heritage. As a person, Francis Lee Jaques was an archetypical American character with pioneer roots, self-taught, independent, and idealistic. Working from his direct experiences, he expressed his love and understanding for nature in his art. Although he lived in New York City for nearly thirty years, he never painted it. Whereas he spent his life painting animals, almost never is there a cat, dog, cow or other domestic animal in his work. Instead he sought out places and beings less dominated by humanity; places where people were visitors or direct dependents of nature. This wilderness he painted for its own intrinsic beauty and significance, and for the values he found there. Lee Jaques's achievement was the expression in visual art of an American wilderness ethic.

Bibliography

Barton, D. R., "Odyssey of a Bird Artist," Natural History. May 1939, pp. 298-308.

Berry, Ana M., *Animals in Art*. London: Chato and Windus; Detroit: Tower Books, 1971.

Clark, Kenneth, *Animals and Men, Their Relationships as Reflected in Western Art from Prehistory to the Present Days*. London: Thames and Hudson, 1977.

Dance, S. Peter, *The Art of Natural History, Animal Illustrators and Their Work*. Woodstock, New York: Overlook Press, 1978.

Eckelberry, Don R., "Birds in Art and Illustration." *The Living Bird*, 2nd Annual of the Cornell Laboratory of Ornithology, 1963, pp. 69-83.

Eckelberry, Don R., "The Artistry of F. L. Jaques," *Naturalist*, 1970, vol. 21, no. 1, pp. 8-10.

Eckelberry, Don R., "Of Animals and Art." *Audubon*, September 1978, vol. 80, no. 5, p. 105.

Goodrich, Lloyd, *Winslow Homer*. New York: George Braziller, Inc., 1959.

Hill, Martha, "Liljefors of Sweden: the Peerless Eye." *Audubon*, September 1978, vol. 80, no. 5, pp. 70-104.

Huth, Hans, *Nature and the American, 3 Centuries of Changing Attitudes*. Berkeley and Los Angeles: University of California Press, 1957.

Jaques, Florence Page, *Francis Lee Jaques, Artist of the Wilderness World*. New York: Doubleday and Co., Inc., 1973.

Jaques, Florence Page, *Birds Across the Sky*, Harper Brothers, 1942.

Lanes, Selma, "The Brandywine Legacy." *Portfolio*, May-June 1981, pp. 70-77.

Larson, Robert G., "F. L. Jaques, His Artistry and Influence," *Naturalist*, 1970, vol. 21, no. 1, pp. 2-7.

Larson, Robert, "Francis Lee Jaques, The Interpreter of Nature's Realm," *Quarterly*, Midwest Museum Conference of the A.A.M., 1974, vol. 34, no. 2, Spring, n.d.

Marcham, Frederich George, *Louis Agassiz Fuertes and the Singular Beauty of Birds*. New York: Harper and Row, 1971.

Mengel, Robert N., "Beauty and the Beast: Natural History and Art." *The Living Bird*, 18th Annual of the Cornell Laboratory of Ornithology, Itasca, New York, 1979-80, pp. 227-71.

Meyer, Susan E., *America's Great Illustrators*. New York: Harry Abrams, Inc., 1978.

Nash, Roderick, *Wilderness and the American Mind*. New Haven, Connecticut: Yale University, 1973.

New York Kennedy Galleries, Inc. *Exhibition of Wildlife and Sporting Watercolors and Paintings*, May 1976.

Norelli, Martina R., *American Wildlife Painting*. New York: Watson-Guptill Publications, 1975.

Novak, Barbara, *American Painting of the 19th Century*. New York: Praeger Publishers, 1969.

Olson, Sigurd, "To the Memory of Francis Lee Jaques." In Florence Page Jaques, *Francis Lee Jaques, Artist of the Wilderness World*. New York: Doubleday & Co., 1973.

Ontario Royal Museum, *Animals in Art*, An International Exhibition of Wildlife Art. Introduction by David M. Lank. Toronto, 1975.

Peattie, Donald Culross, *Green Laurels: The Lives and Achievements of the Great Naturalists*, New York: Garden City Publishing Co., Inc., 1938.

Peterson, Roger Tory, "Bird Painting in America," *Audubon Magazine*, January-February 1950, pp. 26-34.

Peterson, Roger Tory, Foreword to Florence Page Jaques, *Francis Lee Jaques, Artist of the Wilderness World*. New York: Doubleday, 1973.

Stebbins, Theodore E., Jr., *American Master Drawings and Watercolors*. New York: Harper and Row Publishers, 1976.

Teale, Edwin Way, "The Jaques, Artist and Author—Husband and Wife." *Audubon Magazine*, January-February 1950, pp. 26-34.

Vickery, Jim Dale, "Profile of a Pioneer, Francis Lee Jaques." *Backpacking Journal*, Fall 1978, pp. 25-28.

Warmington, Ella, "Artist Jaques. He Loved the North." *St. Paul Pioneer Press* (Sunday) Dec. 12, 1971, p. 1.

Washington National Collection of Fine Arts, Smithsonian Institution, Washington, D.C., *Artist-Naturalists: Observation in the Americas*. Text by Martina Norelli, 1972.

Weekley, Montague, *Thomas Bewick*. London: Oxford University Press, 1953.

Books Illustrated by Francis Lee Jaques

Bailey, A. M. & Niedrach, R. J. *Pictorial Checklist of Colorado Birds*. Denver Museum of Natural History, 1967.

Bolz, J. Arnold. *Portage into the Past*. Univ. of Minnesota Press, 1960.

Bovey, Martin Koon. *The Sage of the Waterfowl*. Wildlife Management Institute, Washington, D.C., 1949.

Bovey, Martin Koon. *Whistling Wings*. New York: Doubleday & Co., Inc., 1947.

Cahalane, Victor H. *Mammals of North America*. Macmillan Co., 1947.

Chapman, Frank M. *My Tropical Air Castle*. D. Appleton-Century, 1929.

Chapman, Frank M. *Life in an Air Castle*. D. Appleton-Century, 1929.

Cruickshank, Helen G. *John & William Bartram's America*. Devin-Adair Co., 1957.

Douglas, William O. *My Wilderness—The Pacific West*. New York: Doubleday & Co., Inc., 1960.

Douglas, William O. *My Wilderness—East to Katahdin*. New York: Doubleday & Co., Inc., 1961.

Garrett, Helen. *Rufous Redtail*. The Viking Press, 1947.

Halle, Louis Joseph, Jr. *Spring in Washington*. New York: William Sloan Associates, Inc., 1947.

Hickey, Joseph J. *A Guide to Birdwatching*. Oxford University Press, 1943.

Howell, Arthur H. *Florida Bird Life*. Florida Dept. of Game & Fish, 1932.

Jaques, Florence Page. *Canoe Country*. Univ. of Minnesota Press, 1938.

Jaques, Florence Page. *The Geese Fly High*. Univ. of Minnesota Press, 1939.

Jaques, Florence Page. *Birds Across the Sky*. Harper Brothers, 1942.

Jaques, Florence Page. *Snowshoe Country*. Univ. of Minnesota Press, 1944.

Jaques, Florence Page. *Canadian Spring*. Harper & Bros., 1947.

Jaques, Florence Page. *As Far as the Yukon*. Harper & Bros., 1951.

Jaques, Florence Page. *There Once Was a Puffin, and Other Nonsense Verses*. Sanbornville, New Hampshire: Wake-Brook House, 1957.

Jaques, Florence Page. *Francis Lee Jaques, Artist of the Wilderness World*. New York: Doubleday & Co., Inc., 1973.

Jaques, E. Parker. *Out-door Reveries*. Kansas City, MO: Burton Publishing Co., 1920.

Jaques, Francis Lee. "Outdoor Life's Gallery of North American Game." New York, 1946.

Mayr, Ernst. *Birds of the Southwest Pacific*. Macmillan Co., 1945.

Murphy, Robert Cushman. *Oceanic Birds of South America*. 2 vols. American Museum of Natural History, 1936.

Naumberg, Elsie. *The Birds of Matte Grosso*. Bulletin of the *American Museum of Natural History*, No. 1, LX, 1930.

O'Kane, Walter Collins. *Beyond the Cabin Door*. West Ridge, NH: Smith Publishing, 1957.

O'Kane, Walter Collins. *The Cabin*. New York: Wake Bookhouse, 1955.

Olson, Sigurd F. *The Singing Wilderness*. New York: Alfred Knopf, 1956.

Olson, Sigurd F. *Listening Point*. New York: Alfred Knopf, 1961.

Olson, Sigurd F. *The Lonely Land*. New York: Alfred Knopf, 1961.

Ripley, Sidney Dillon. *A Paddling of Ducks*. New York: Harcourt Brace, 1957.

Roberts, Thomas S. *The Birds of Minnesota*. 2 vols. Univ. of Minnesota Press, 1932.

Spaulding, Edward S. *The Quail*. Macmillan Co., 1949.

Sprunt, A., & Chamberlain, E. B. *South Carolina Bird Life*. Univ. of South Carolina Press, 1949.

Sprunt, Alexander. *Florida Bird Life*. 1954.

Stover, John. *The Flight of Birds*. 1948.

Sturgis, Bertha. *Field Book of Birds of Panama Canal Zone*. G. P. Putnam's Sons, 1928.

Urner, Charles A. *Christmas Poems of Chas. Anderson Urner, 1925-1937. 1938*.

Von Hagen, Victor W., *South American Zoo*. Julian Messner, Inc., 1946.

Walkenshaw, *The Sandhill Cranes*. 1949.

Wiley, Farida, ed. *John Burrough's America*. Deyon-Adair, 1951.

Donald T. Luce earned an undergraduate degree in zoology and a masters degree in medical and biological illustration at the University of Michigan. He is assistant curator of exhibits at the James Ford Bell Museum of Natural History, University of Minnesota. **Laura M. Andrews**, who has a masters degree in art history and museology from the University of Minnesota, is assistant curator at Minnesota's University Gallery.